Teaching Christ's Children
Baltimore, Maryland

www.tccpublishing.com

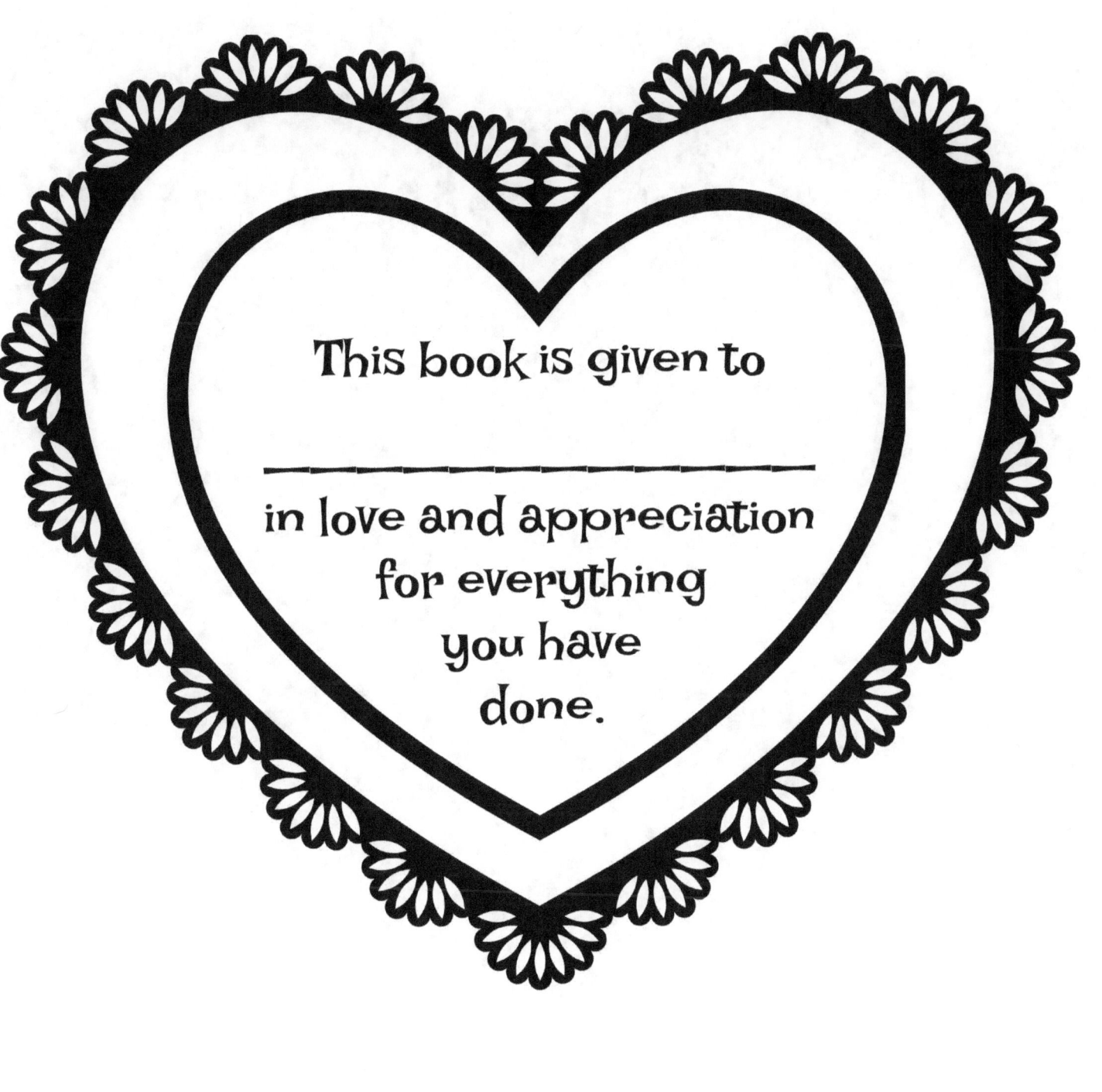

This book is given to

_____

in love and appreciation
for everything
you have
done.

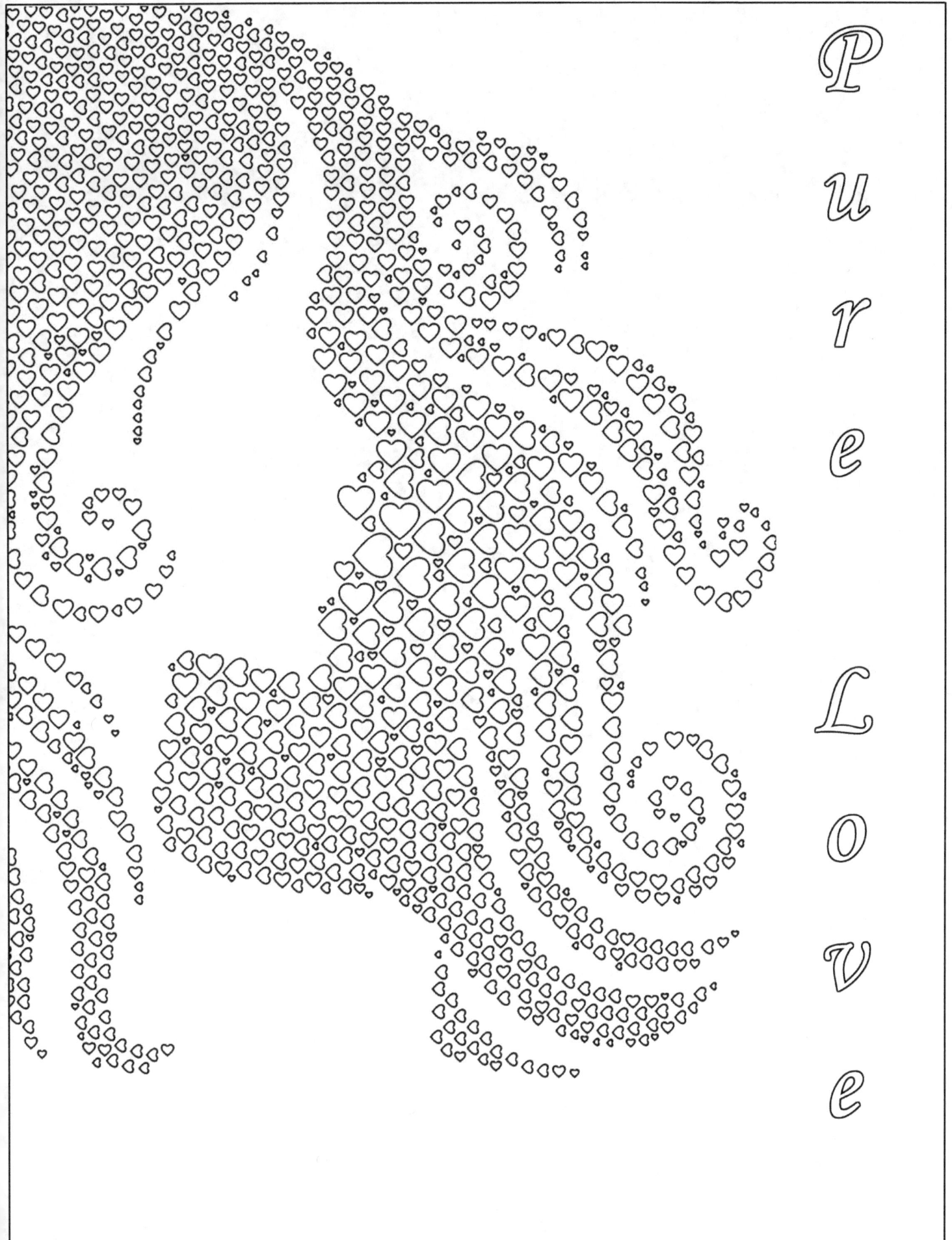

Pure Love

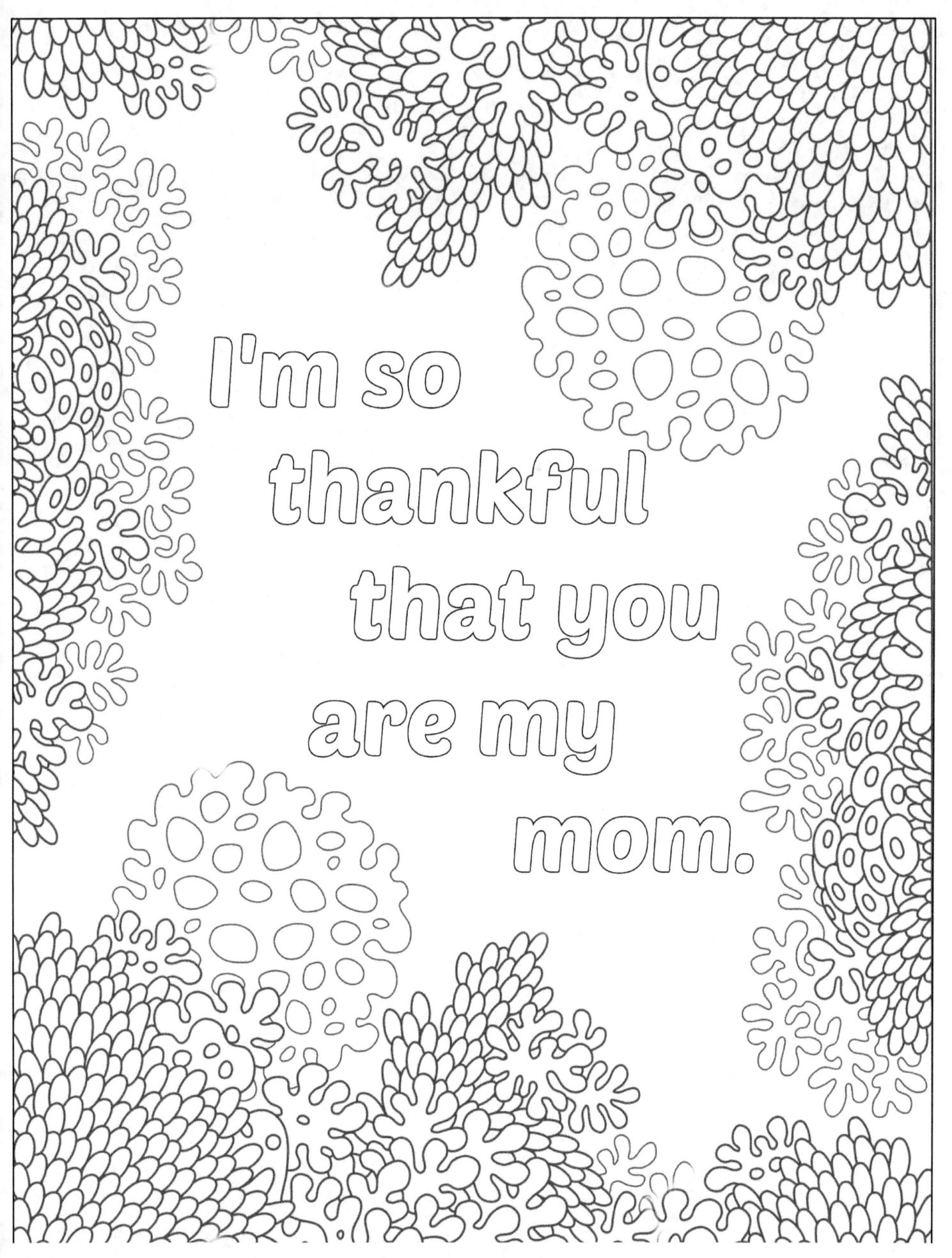

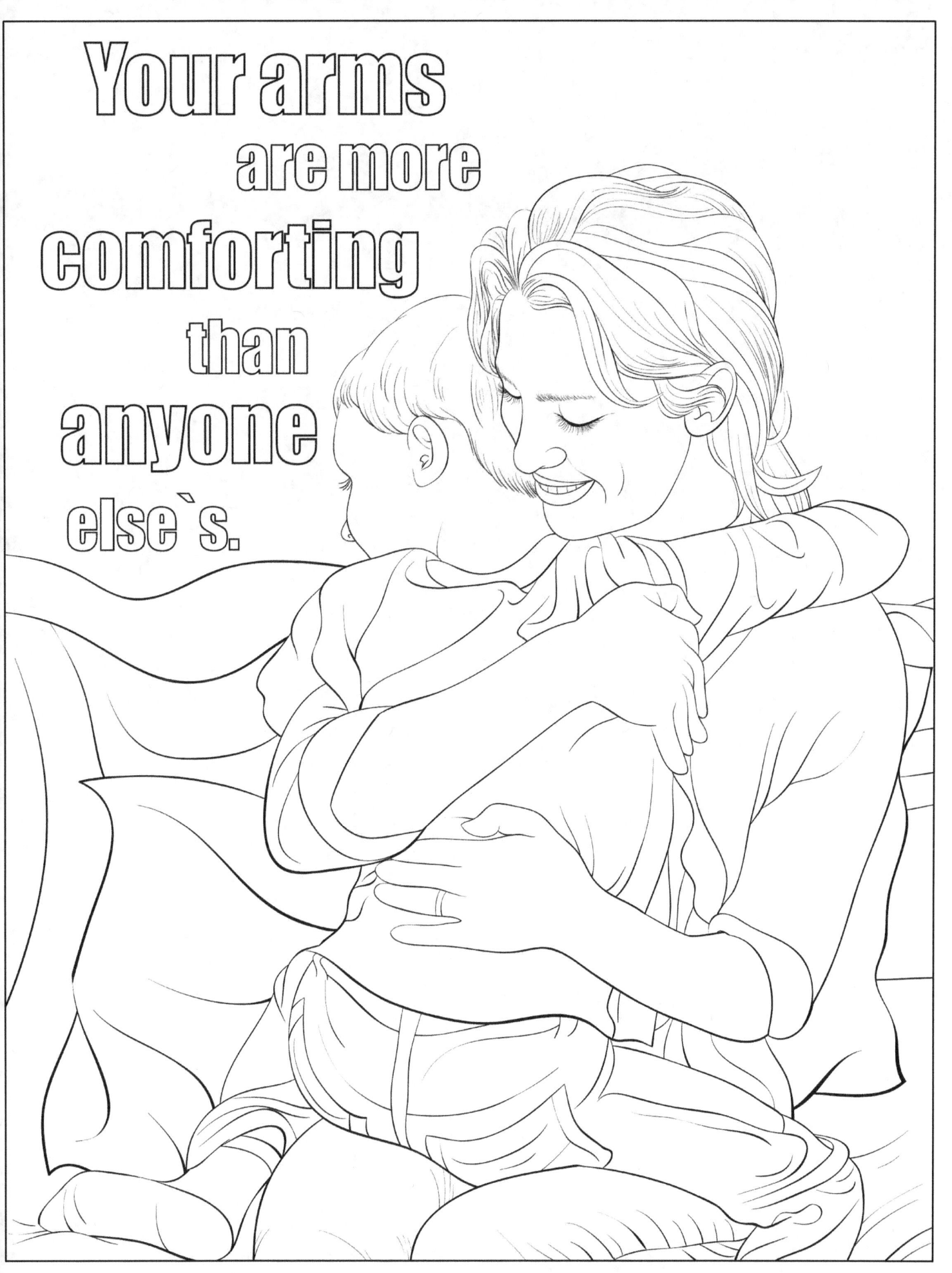

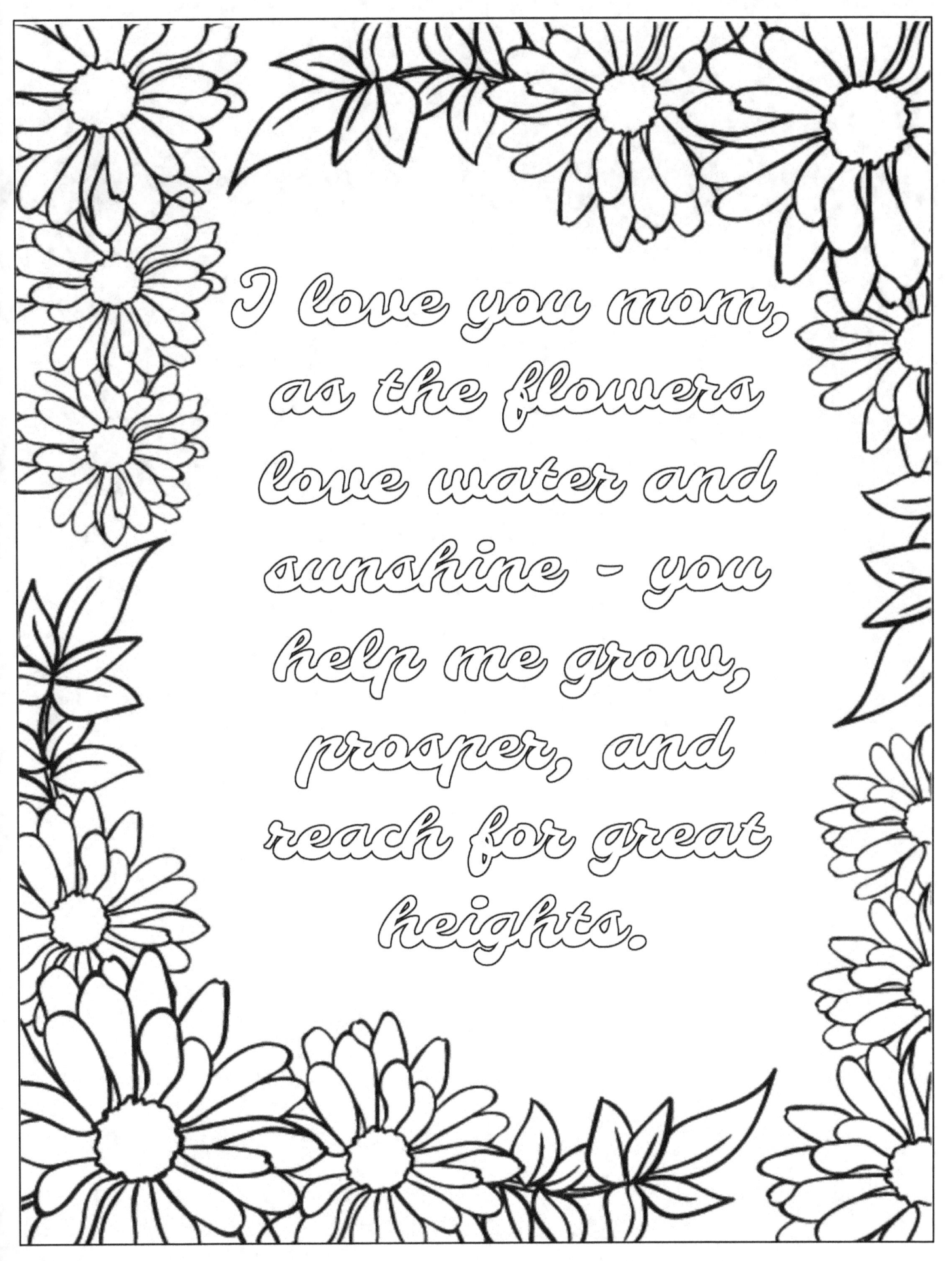

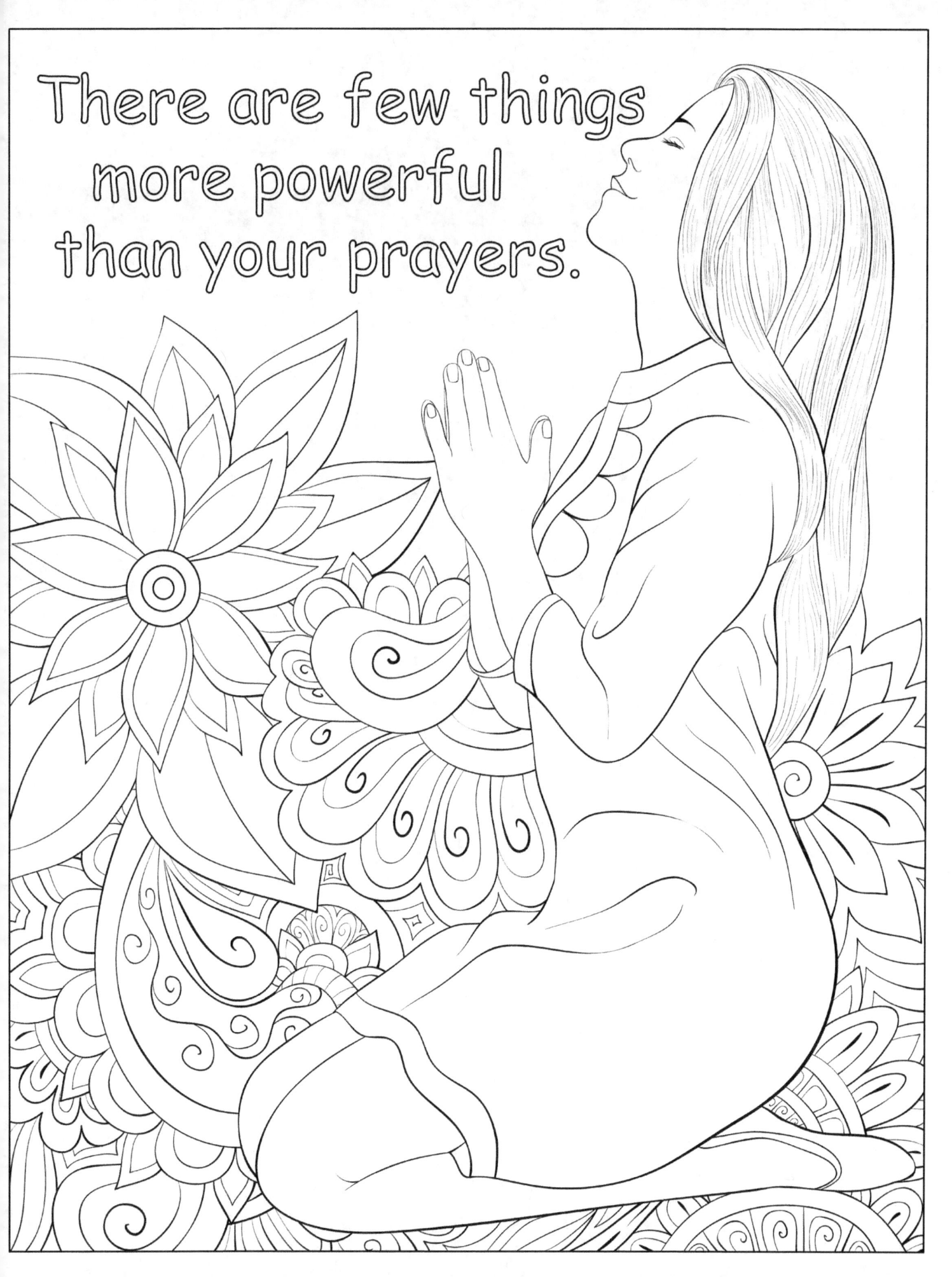

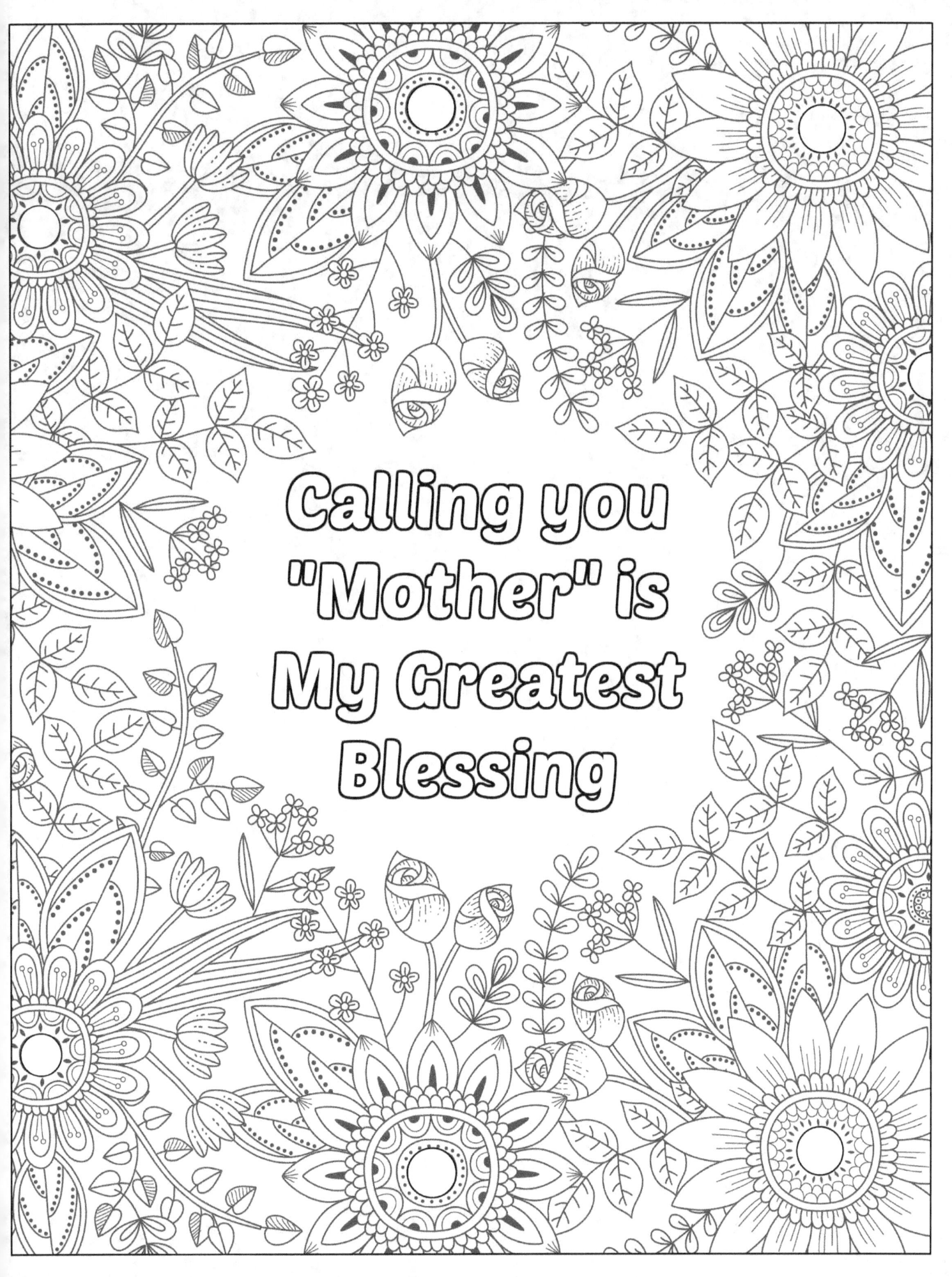

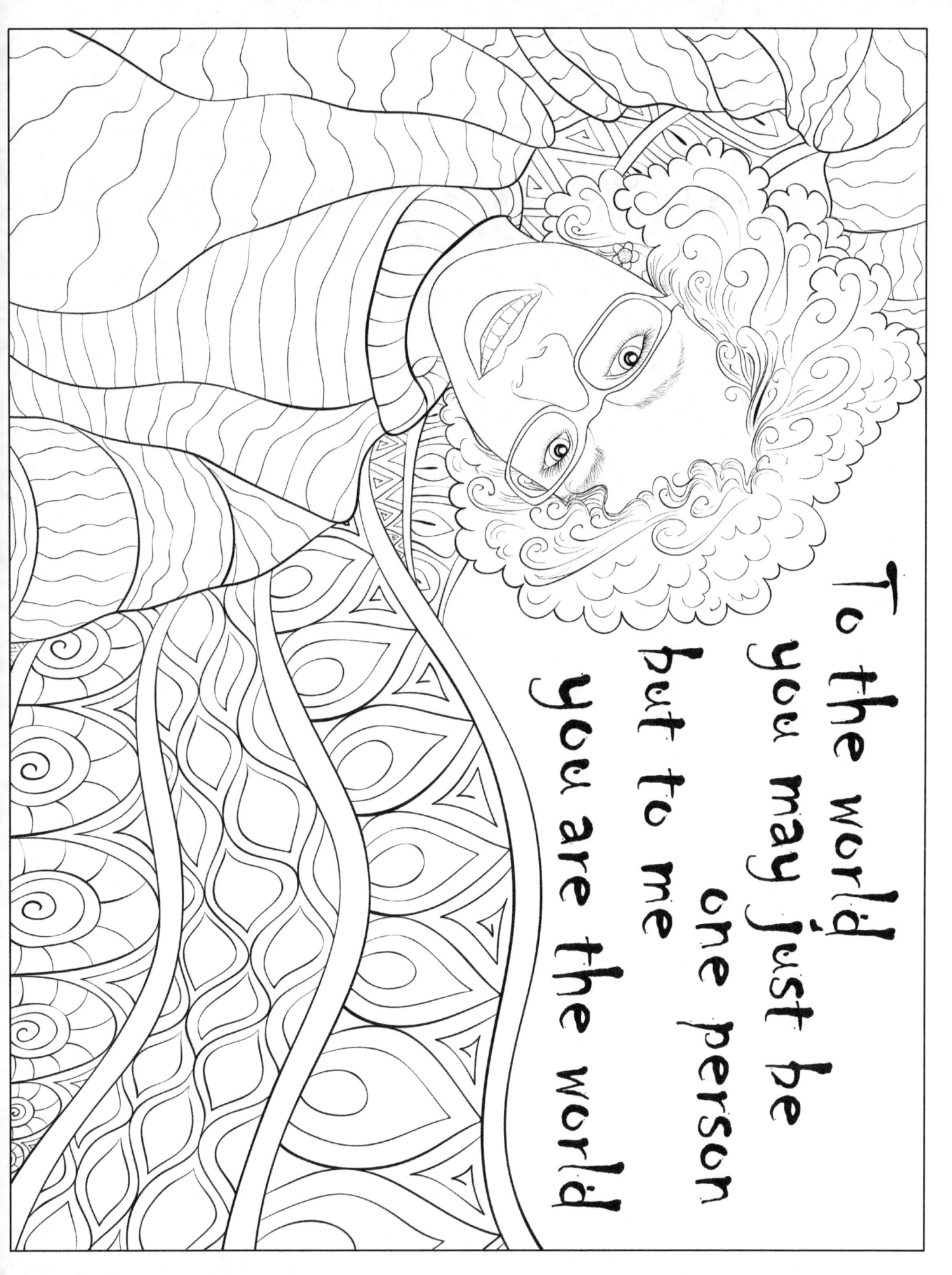

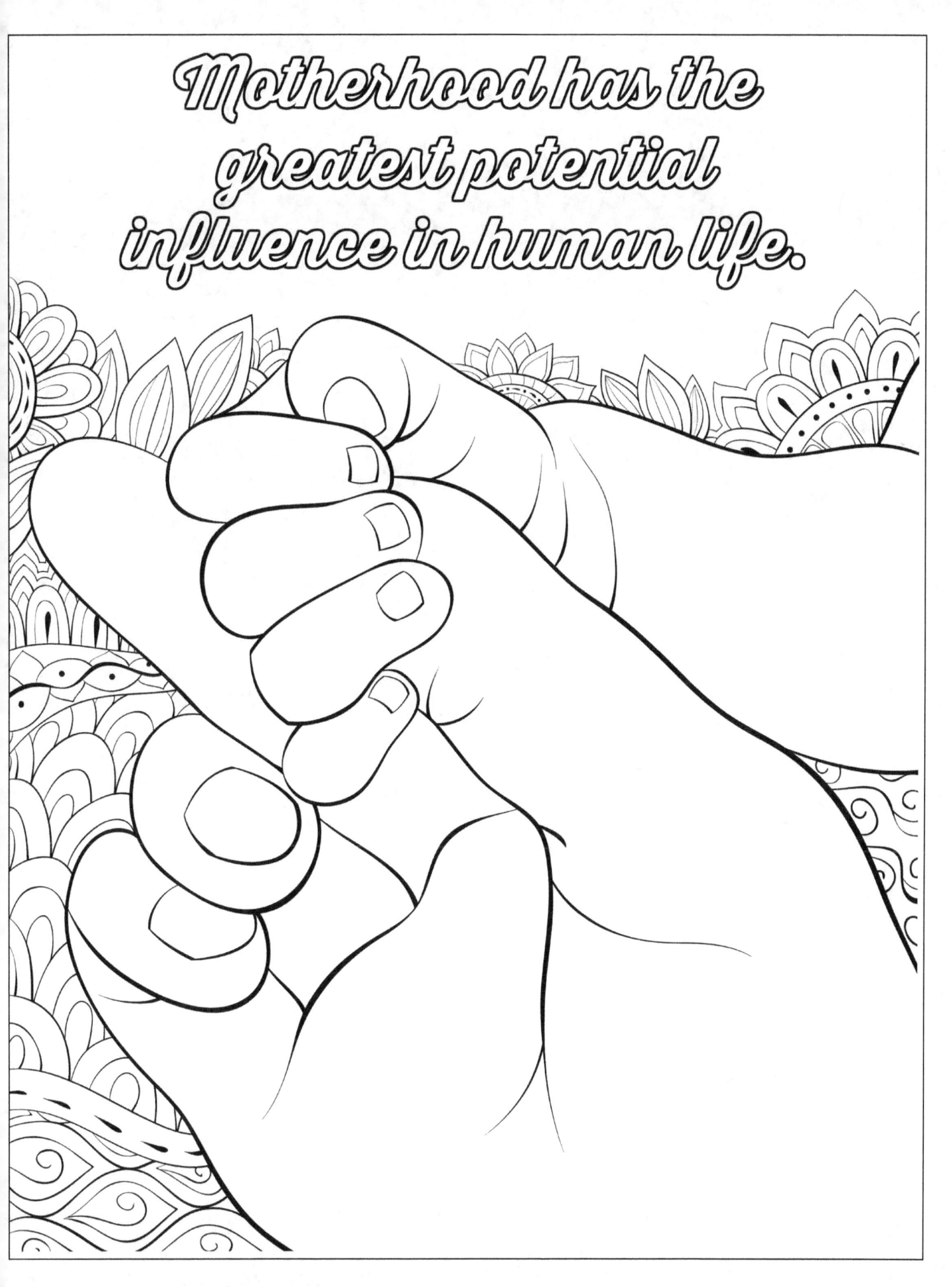

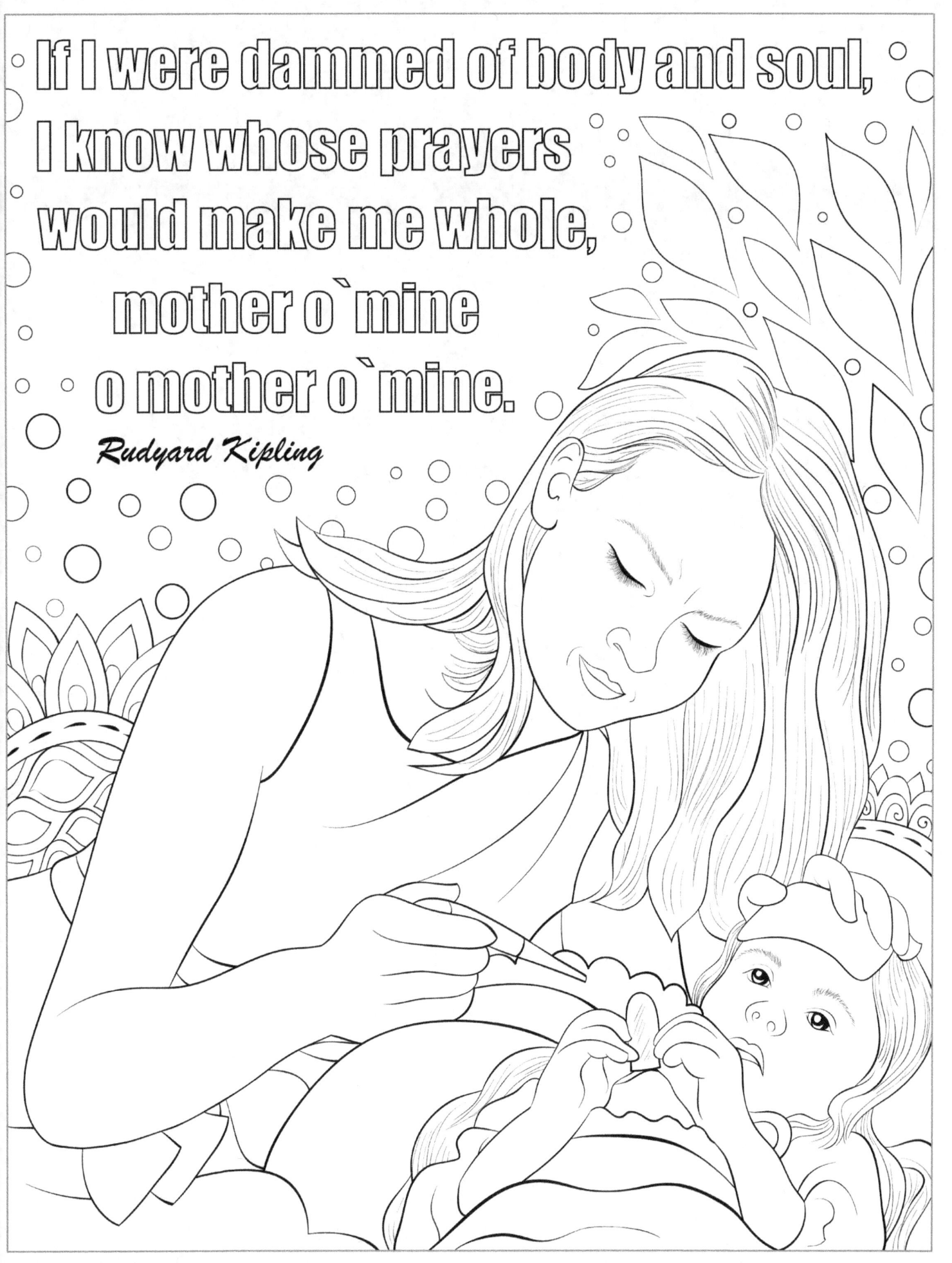

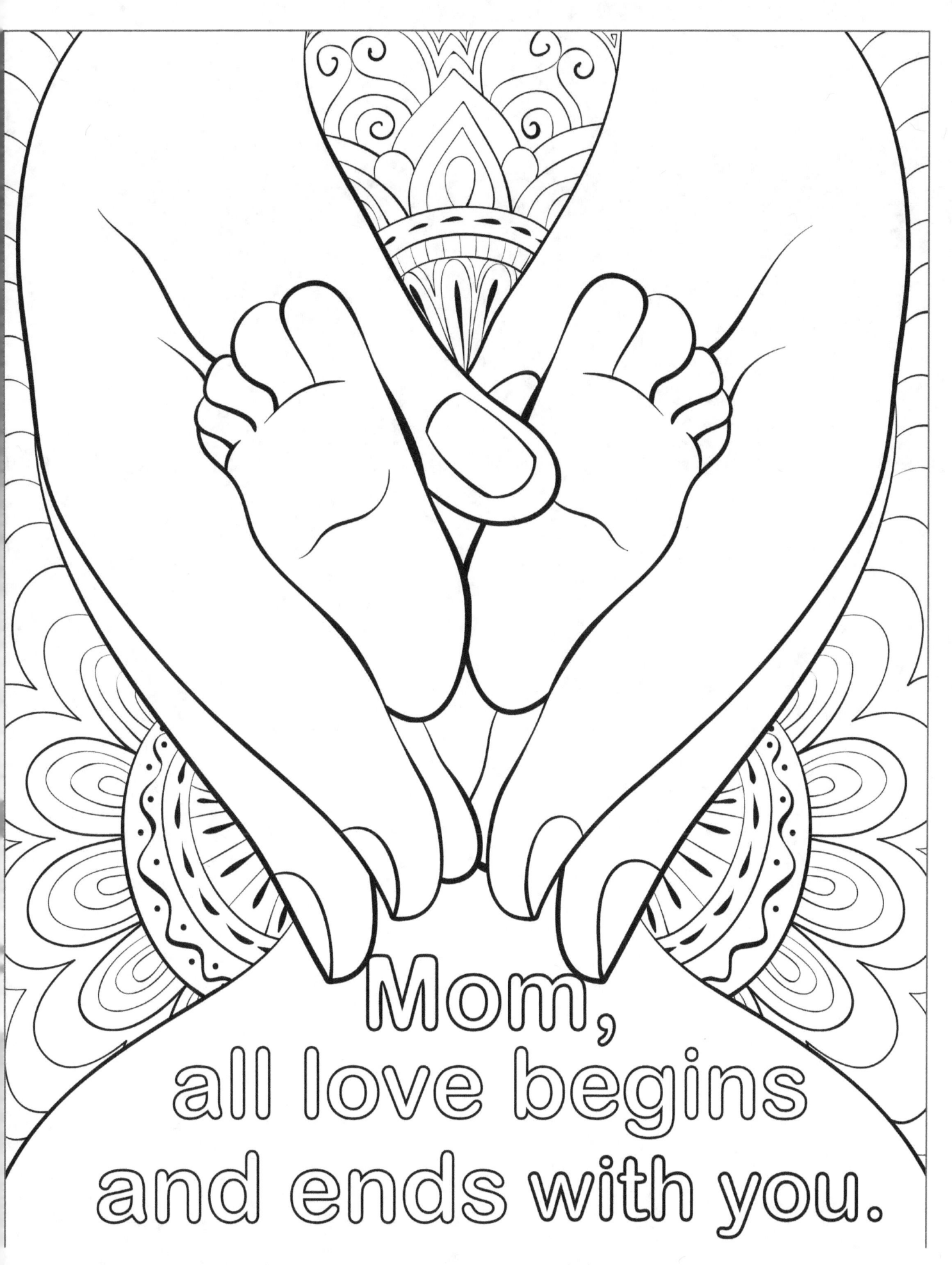

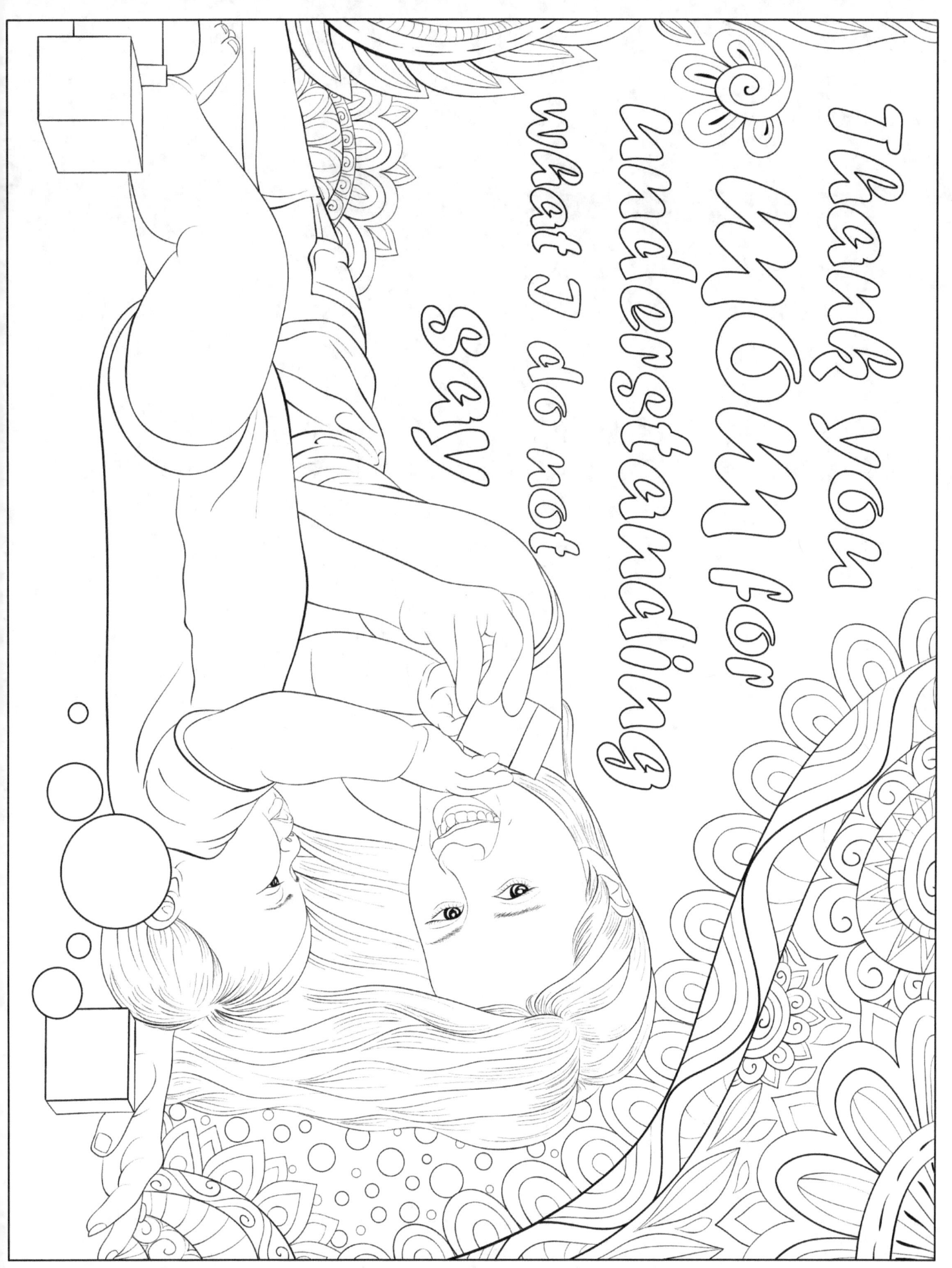

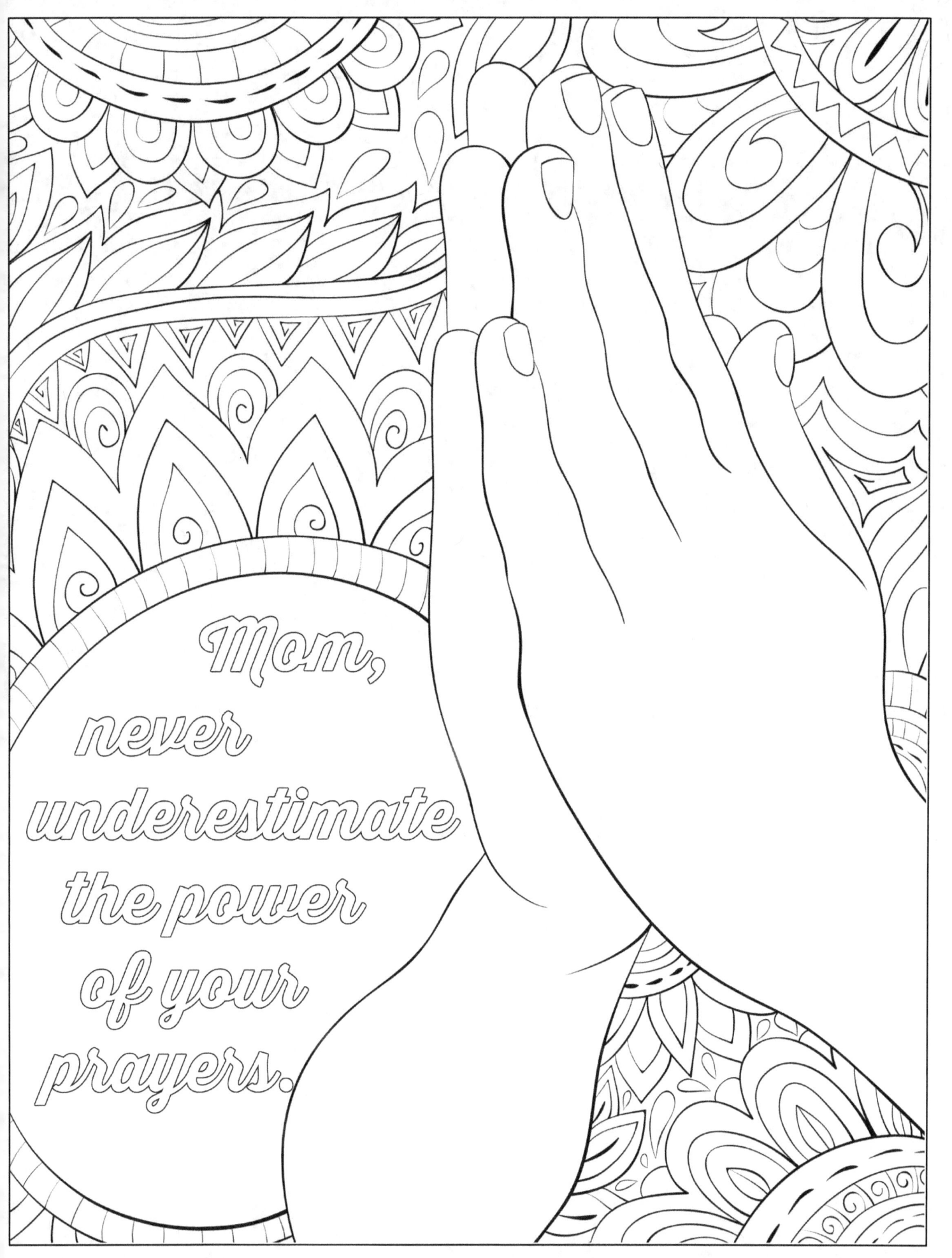

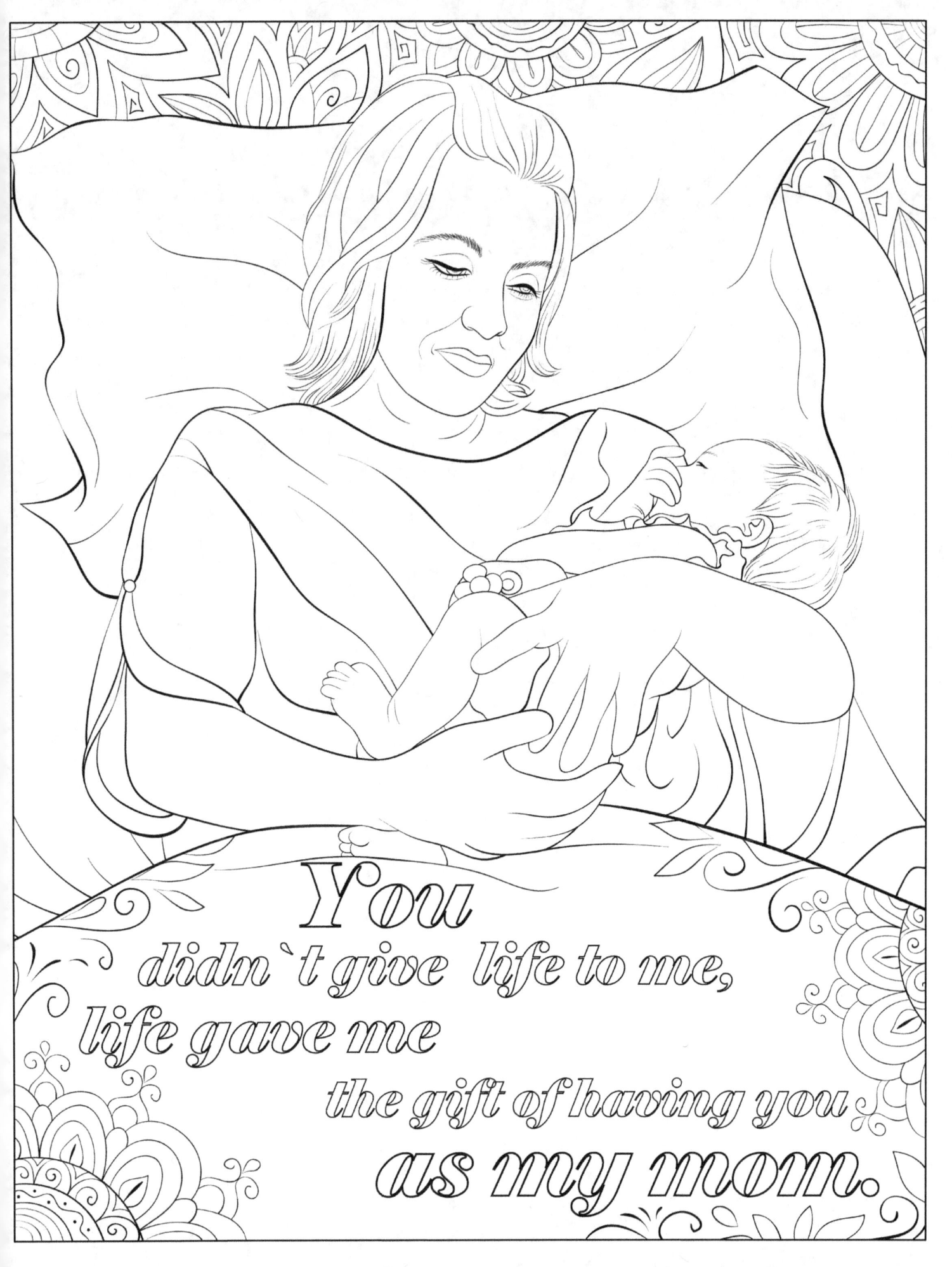

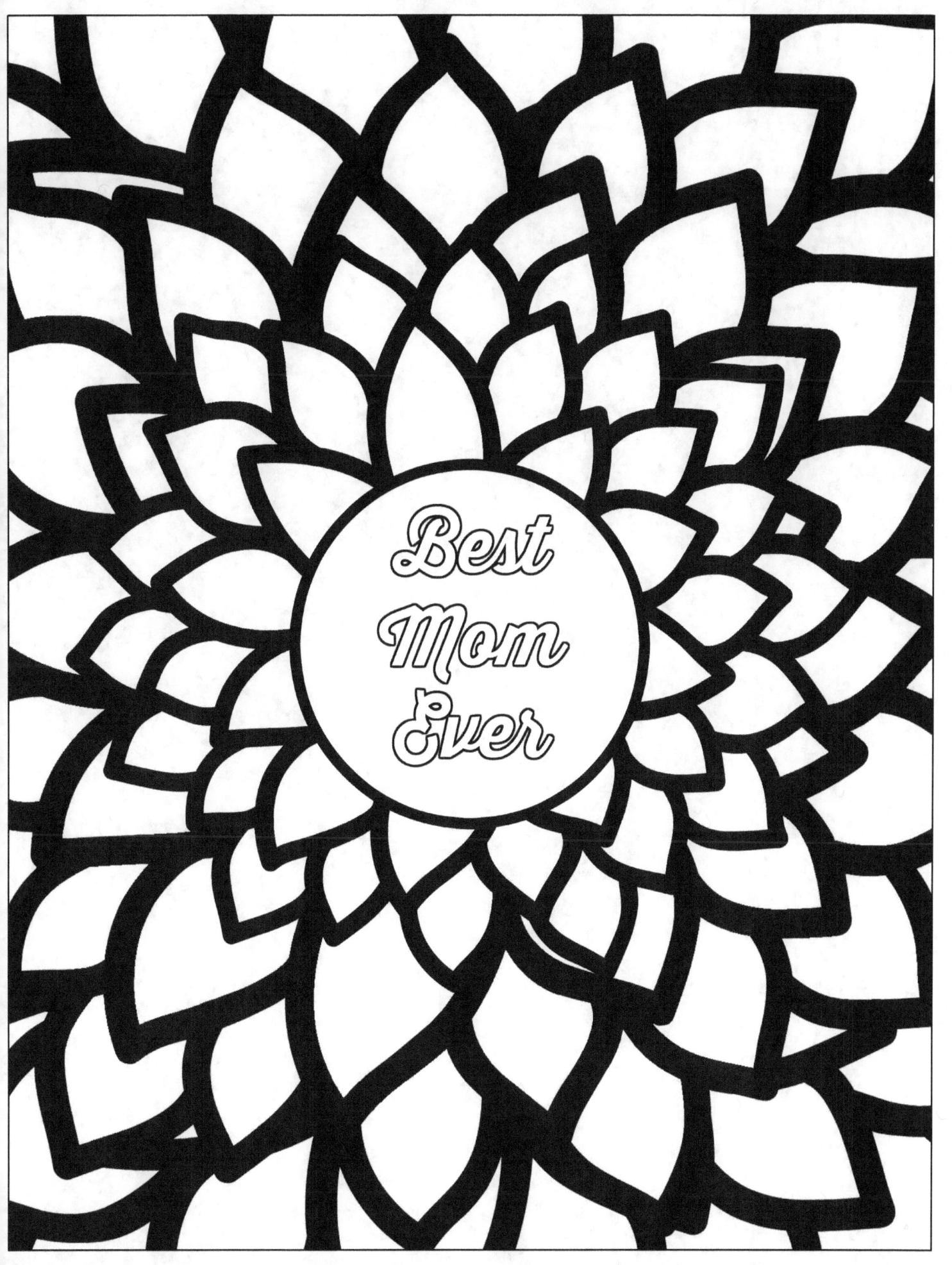

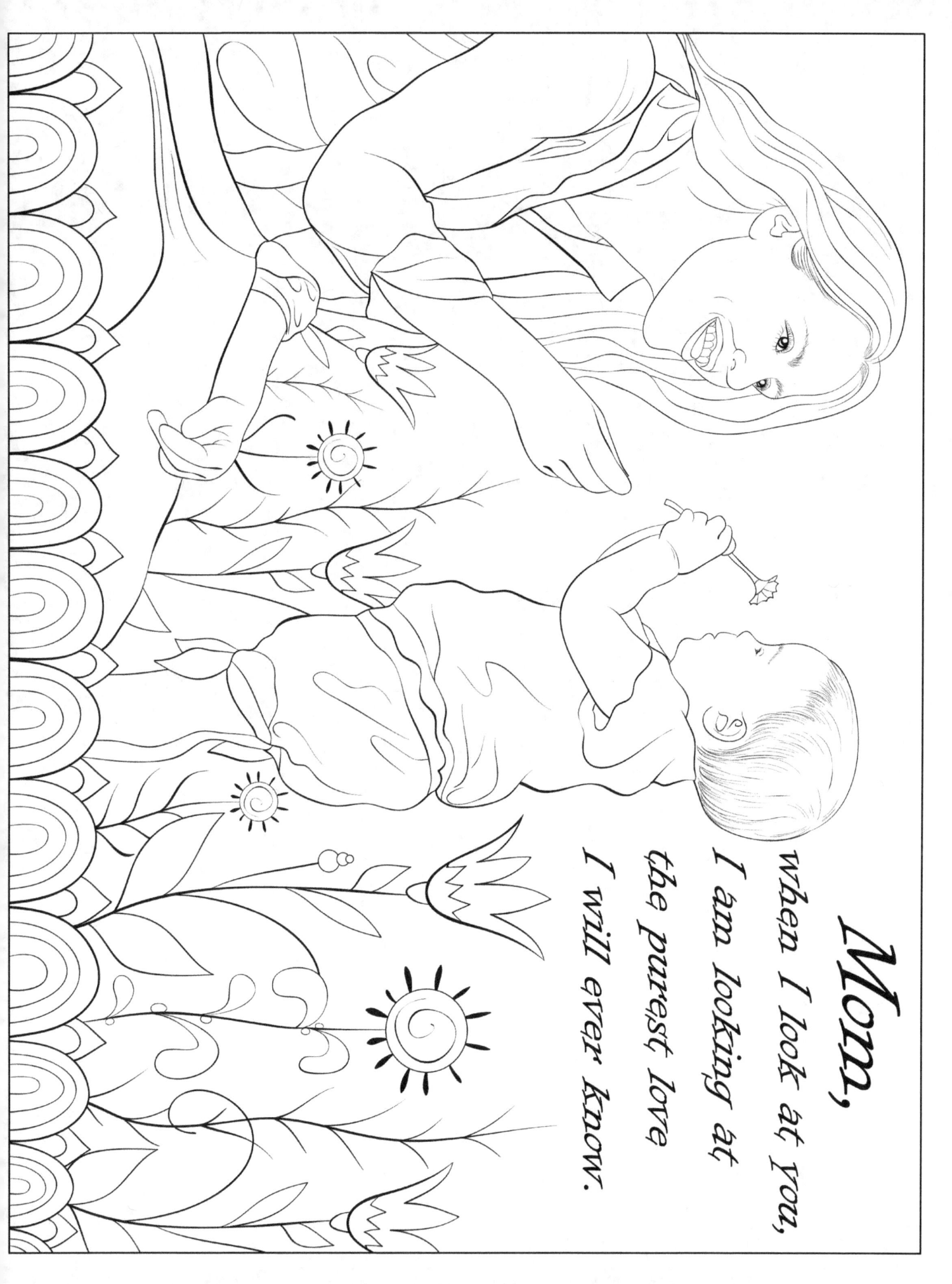

Mom,
when I look at you,
I am looking at
the purest love
I will ever know.

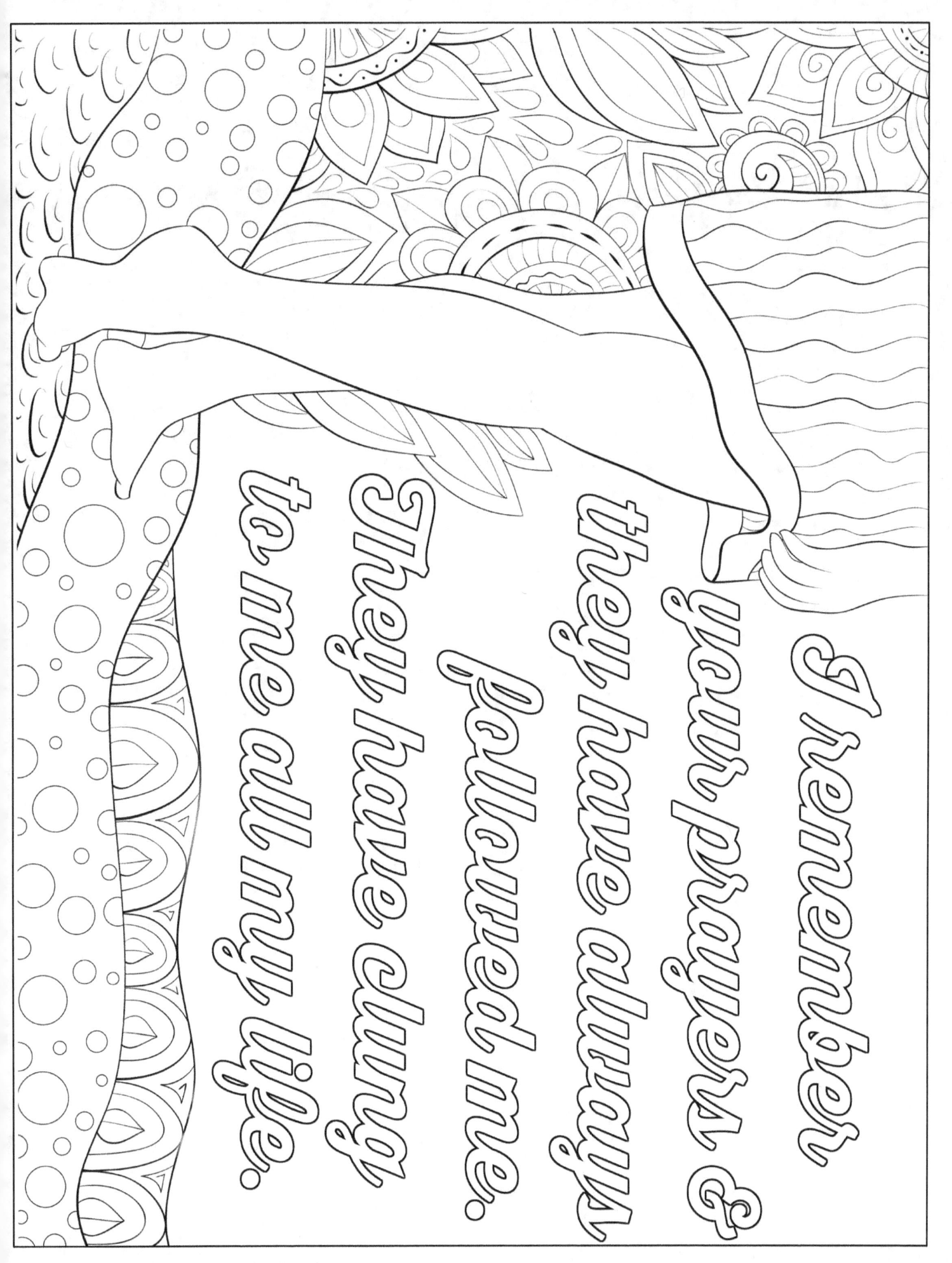

I remember
your prayers &
they have always
followed me.
They have clung
to me all my life.

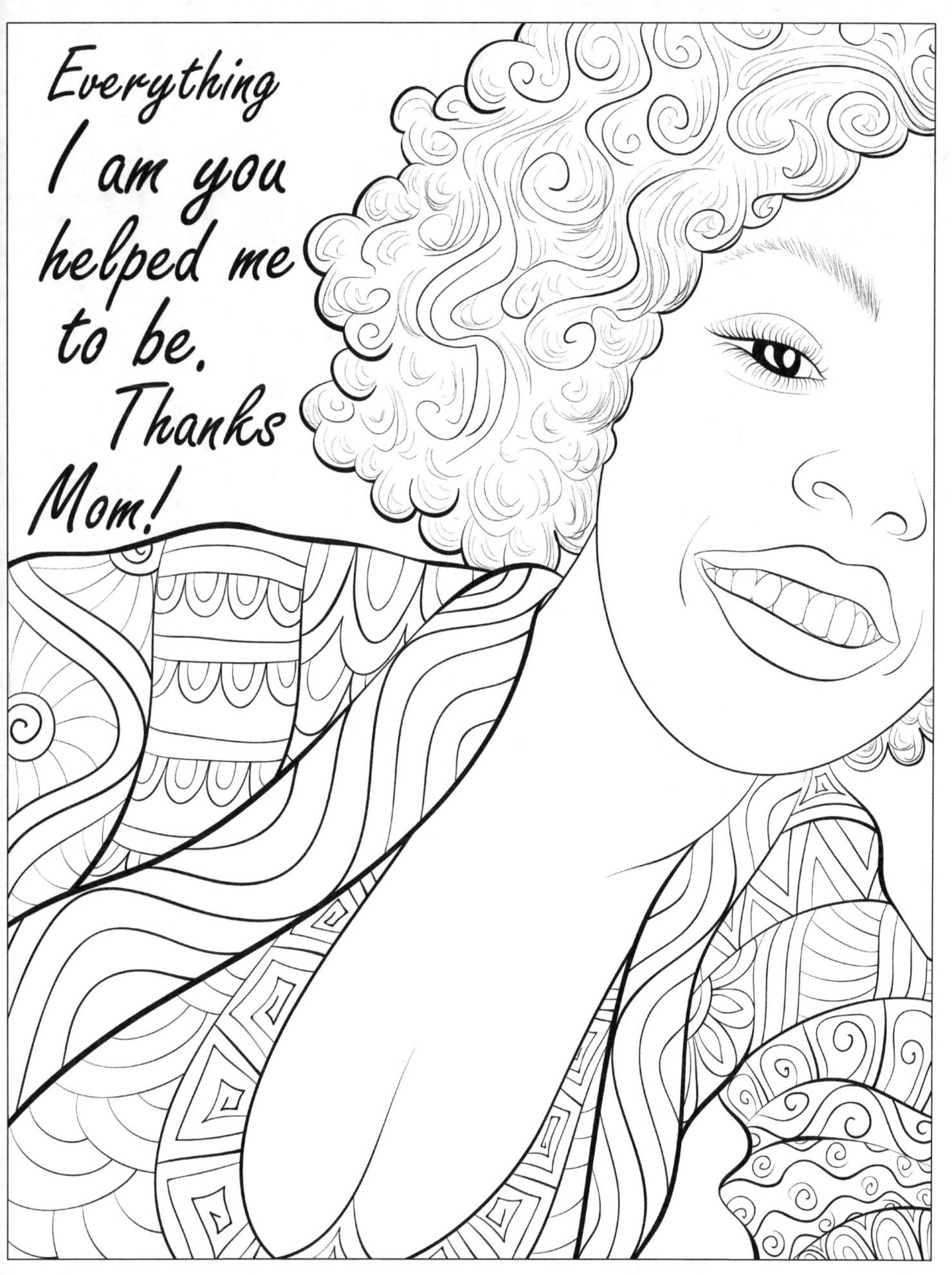

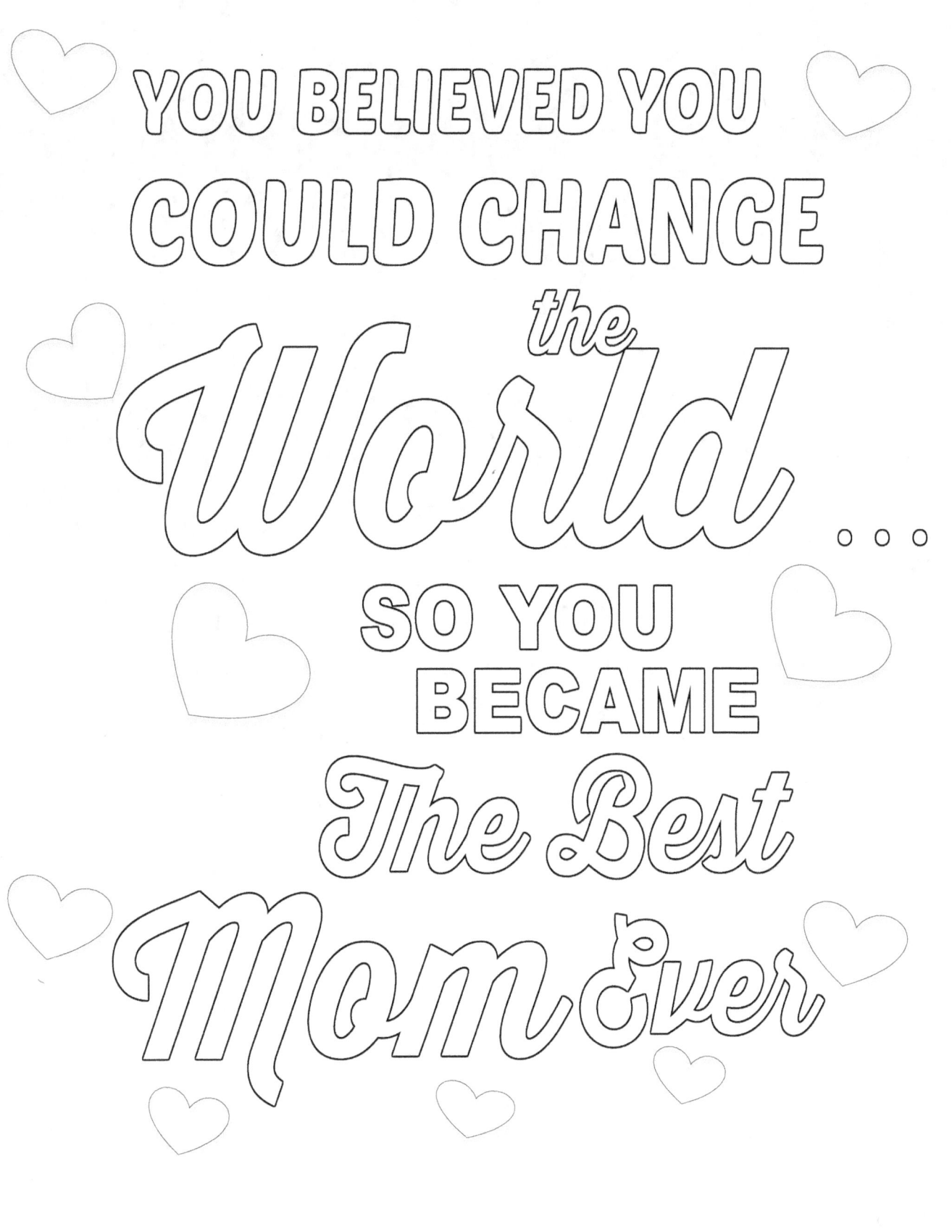

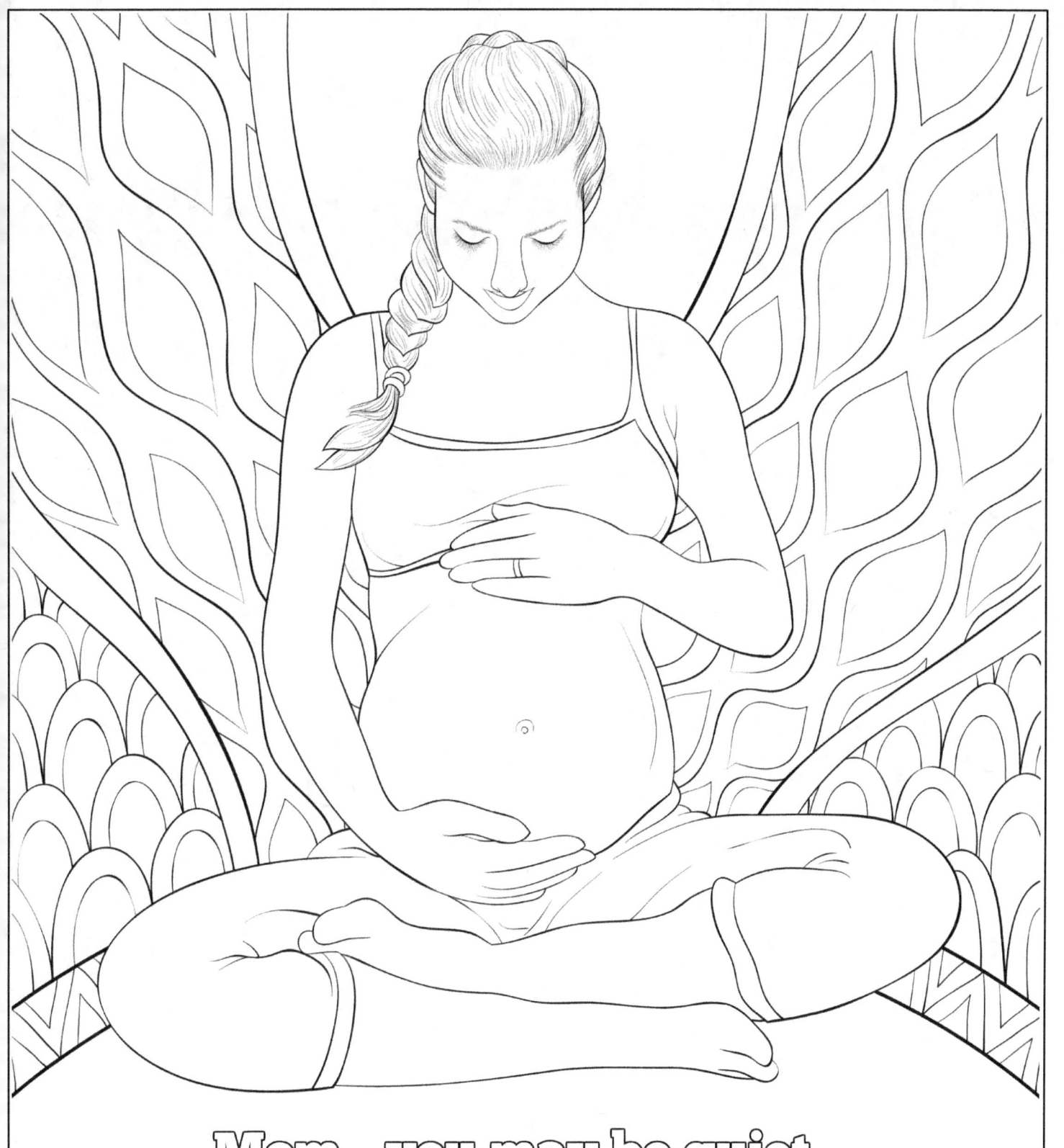

Mom - you may be quiet,
but you are a warrior
and your prayers can move mountains.

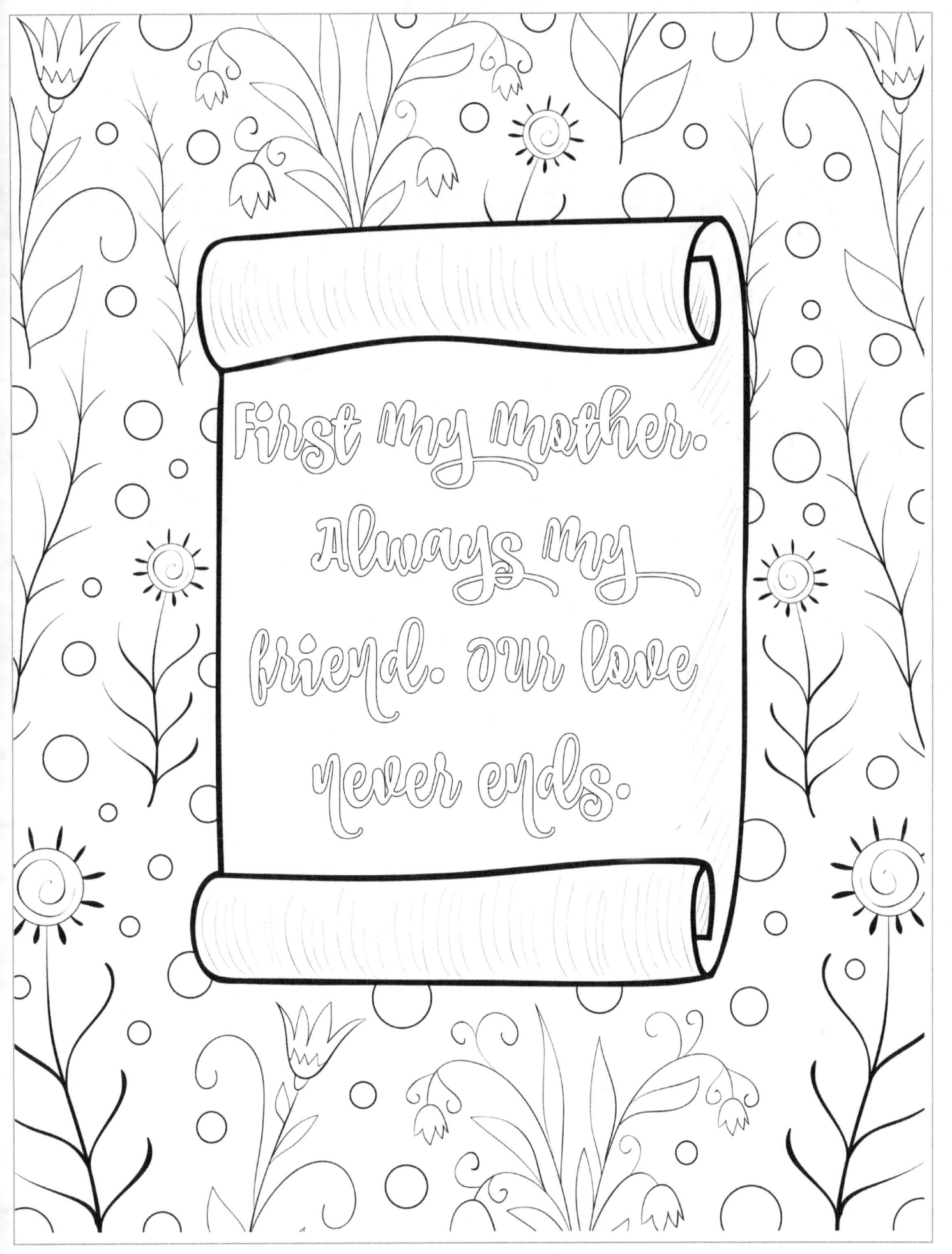

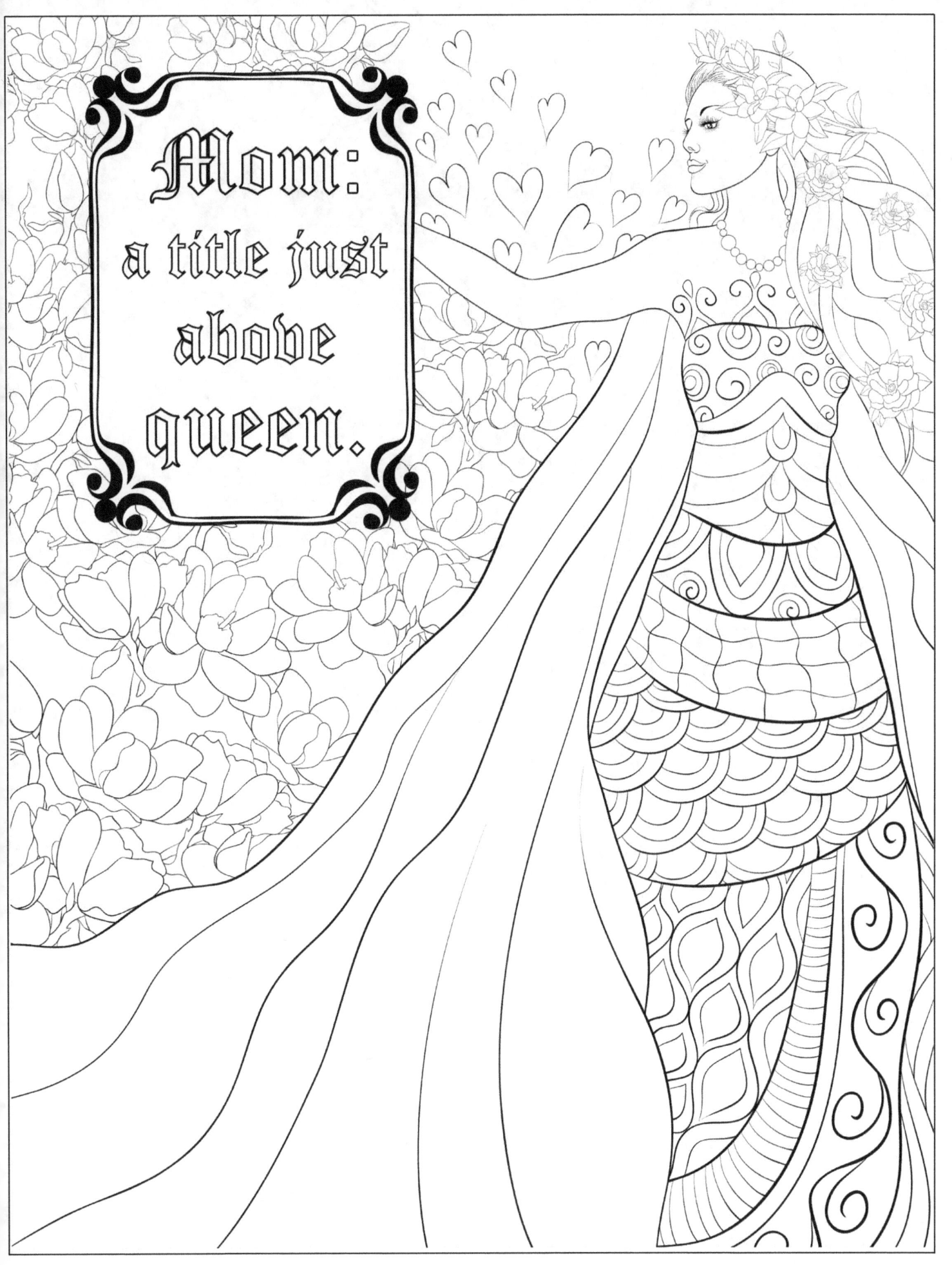

Mom:
a title just
above
queen.

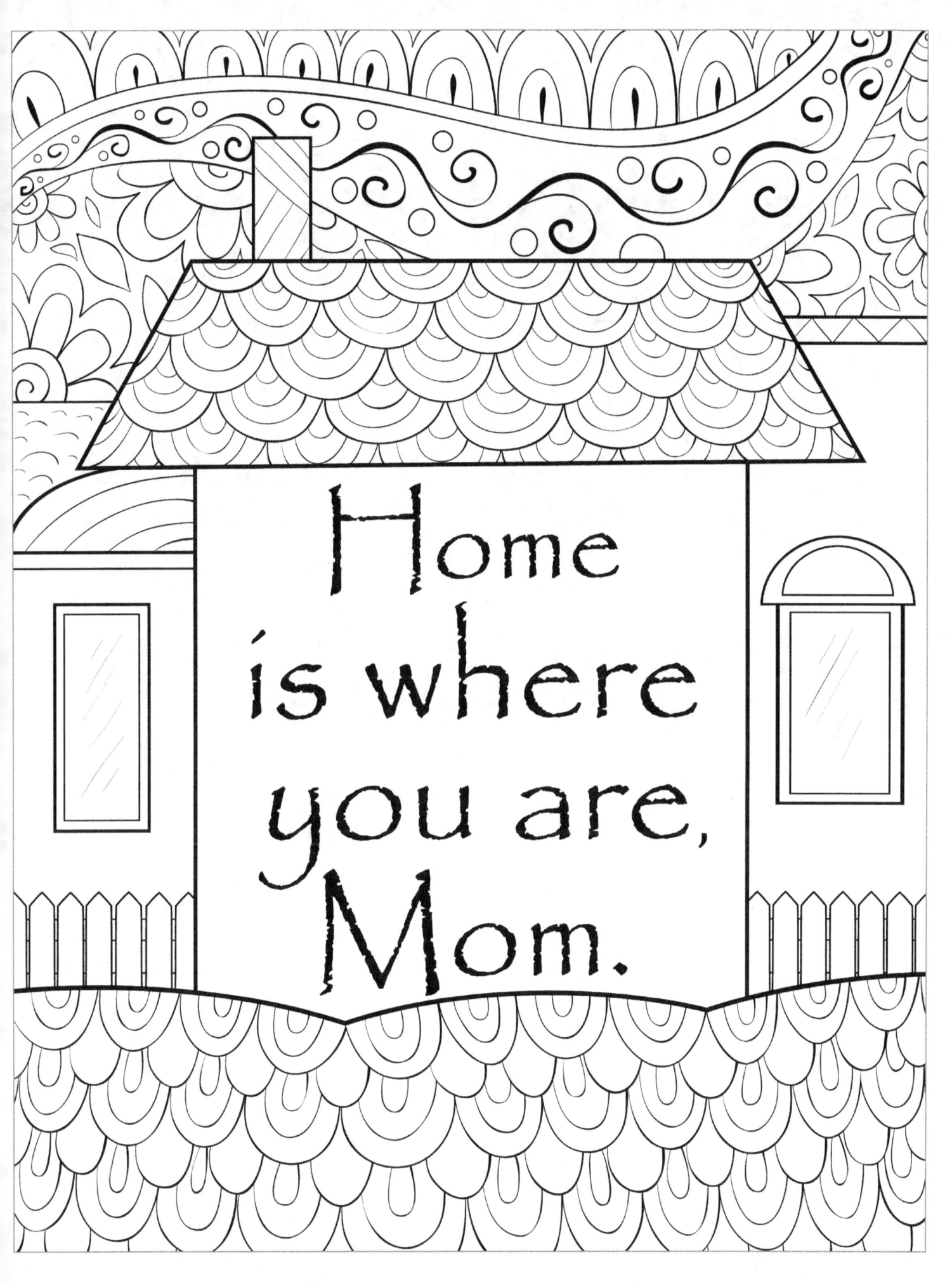

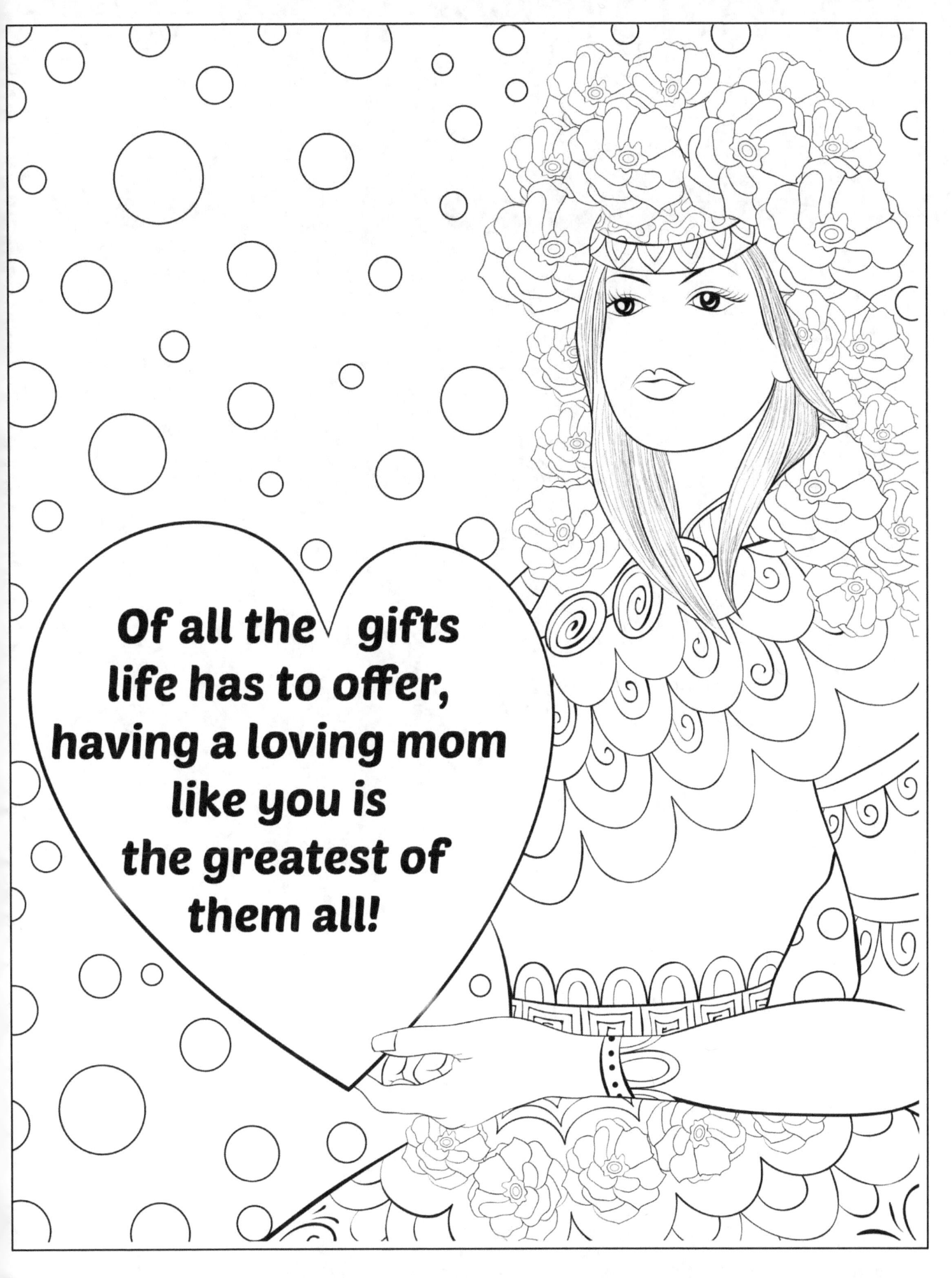

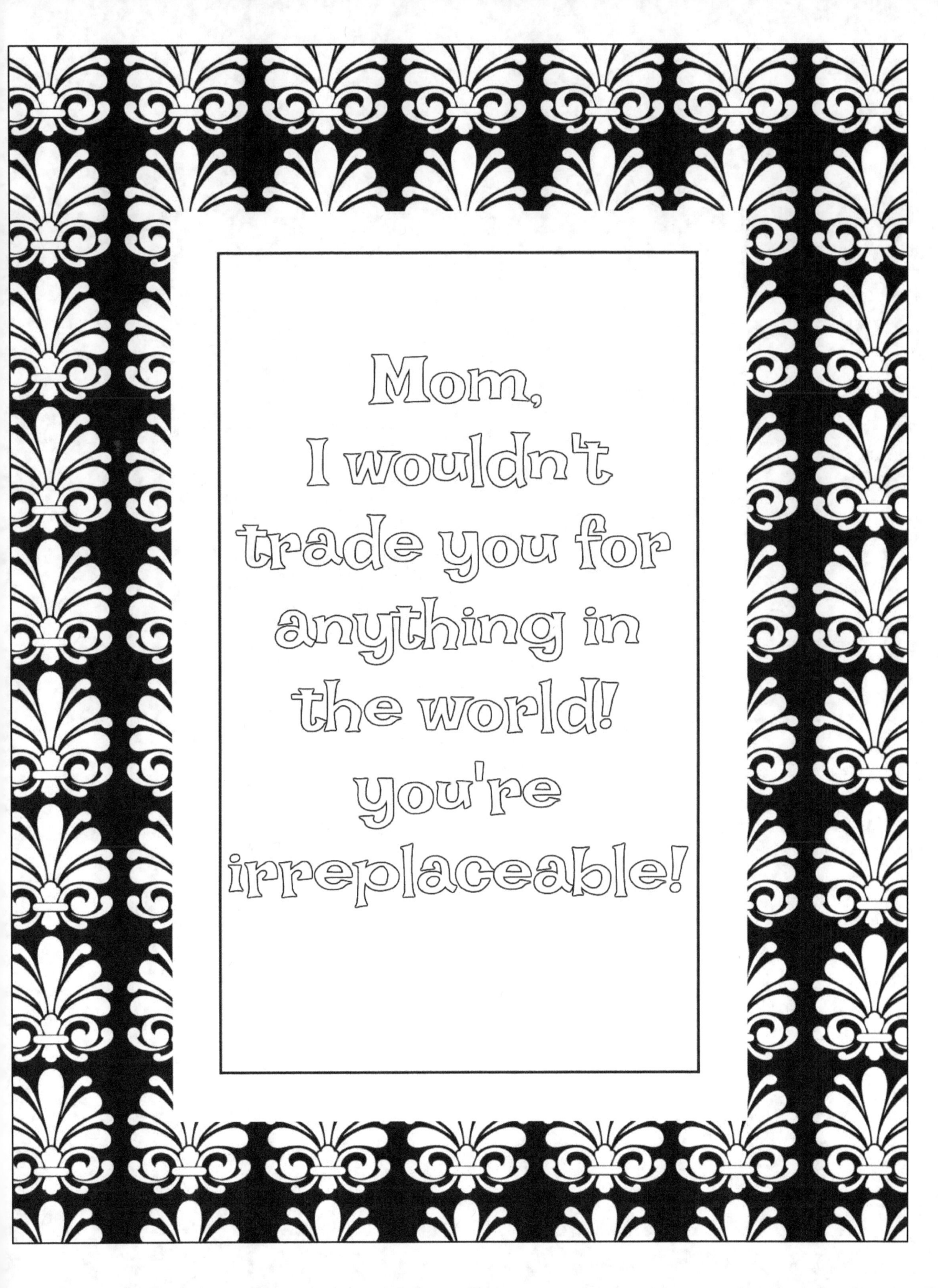

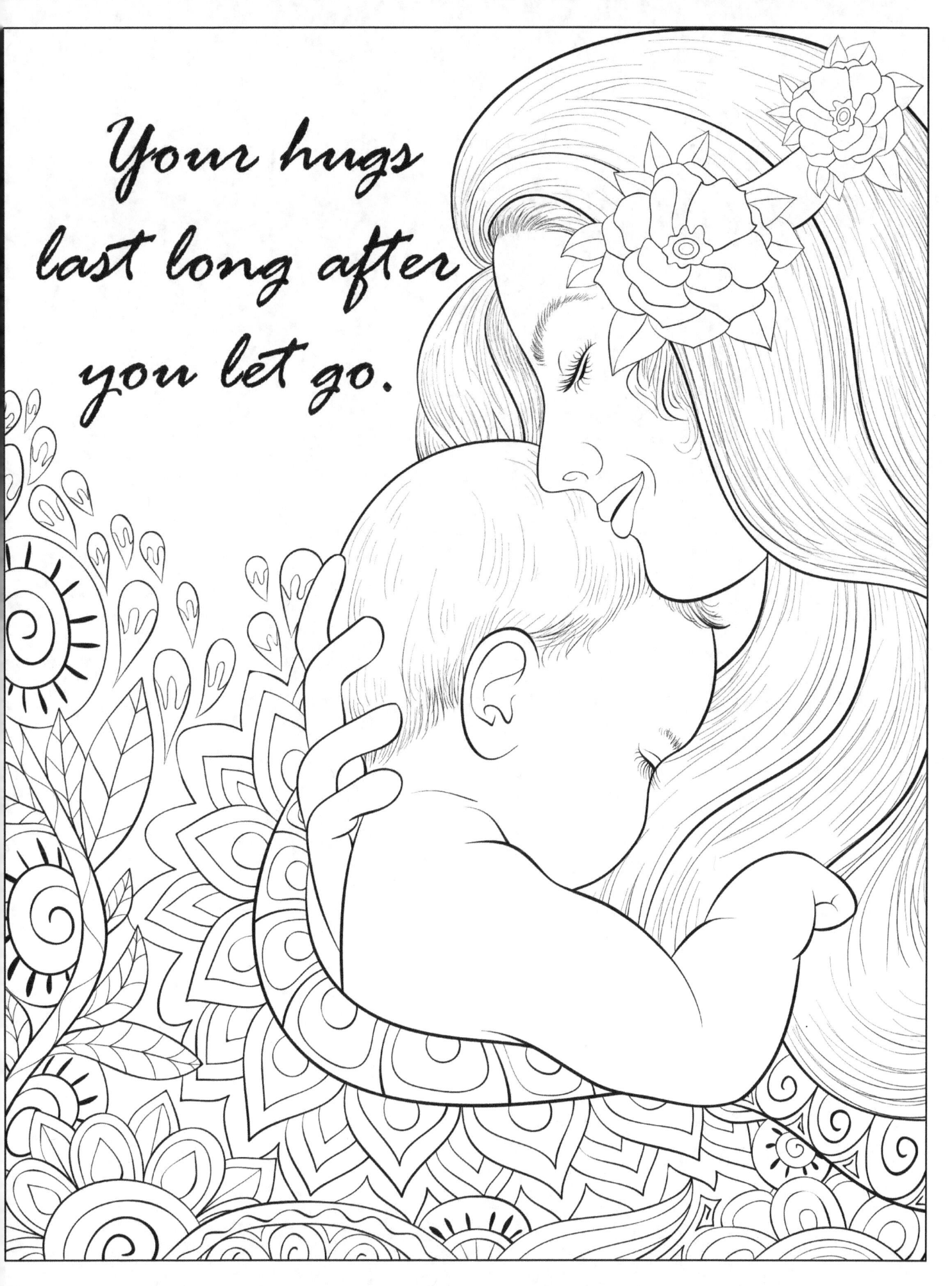

Your hugs
last long after
you let go.

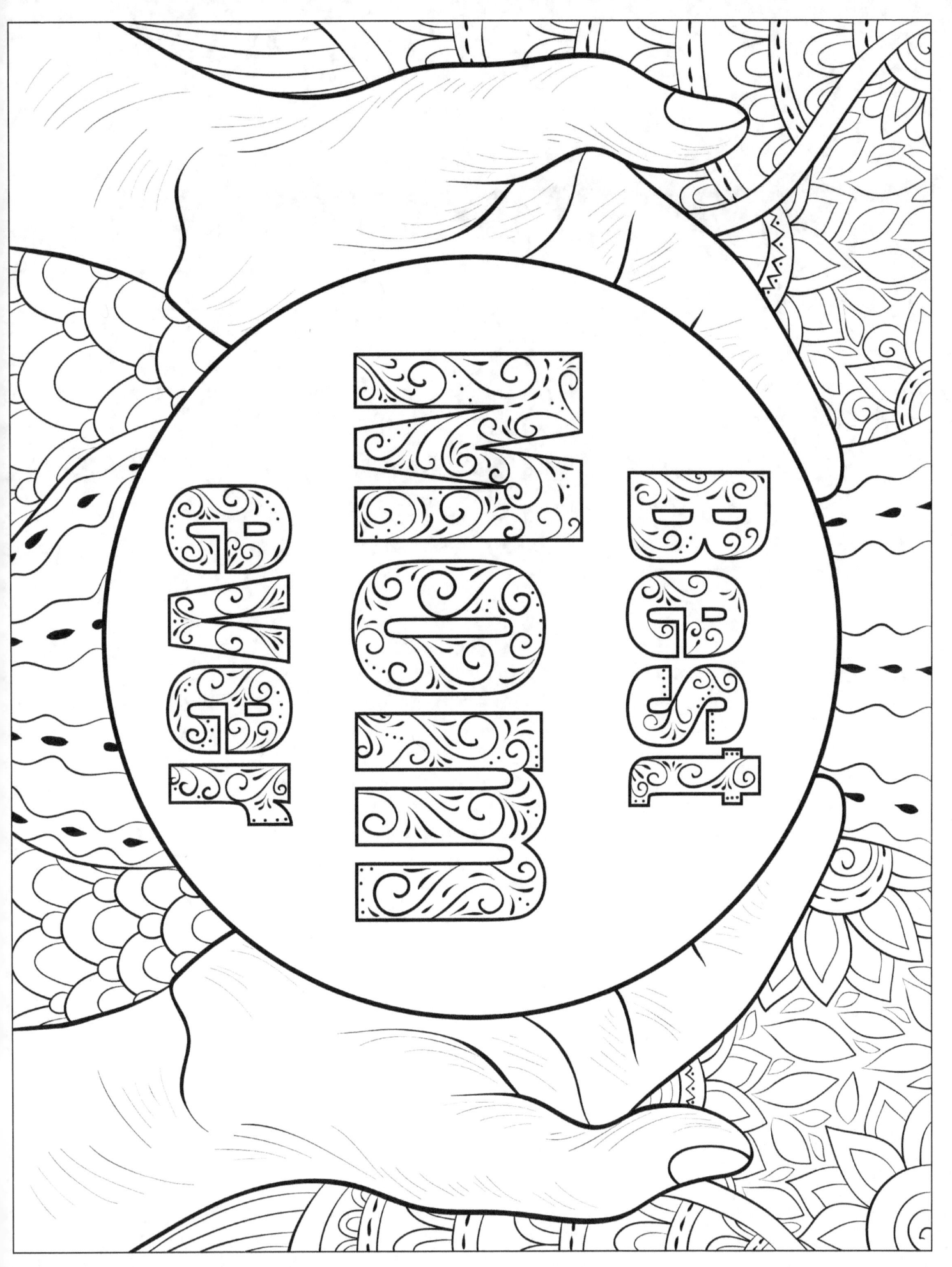

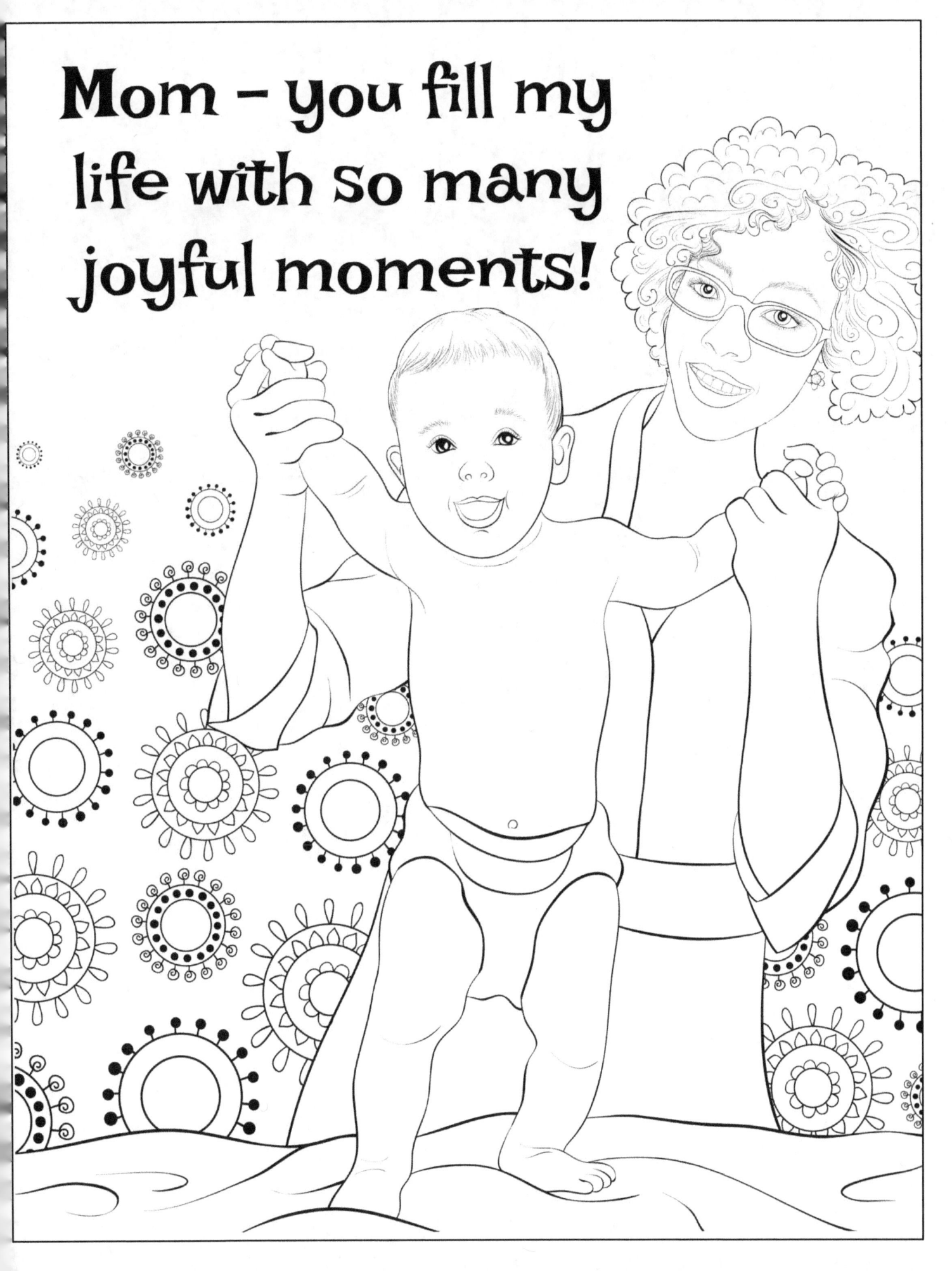

Mom - you fill my life with so many joyful moments!

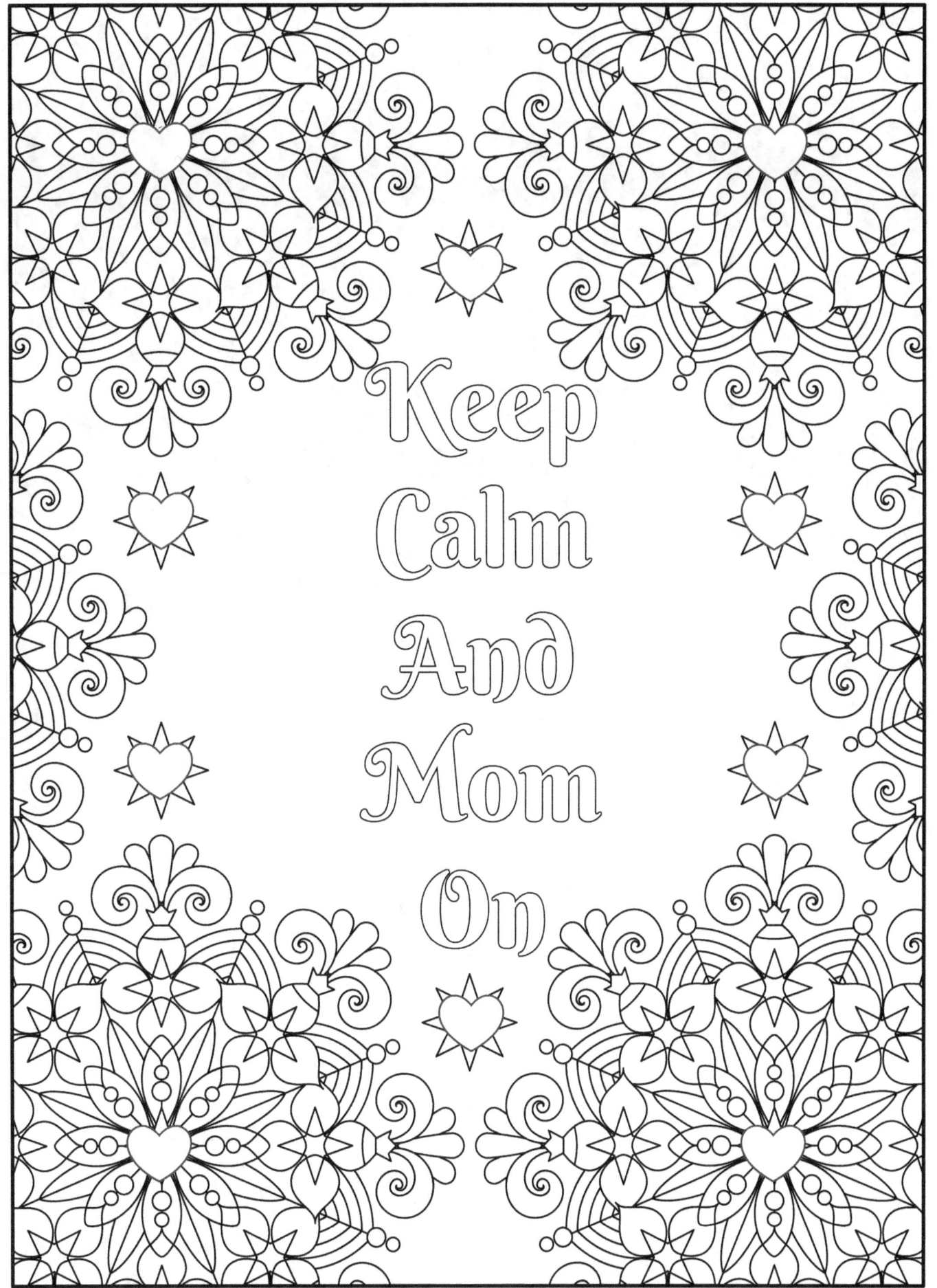

Life doesn't come with a
Manual. It comes with a
Mom.

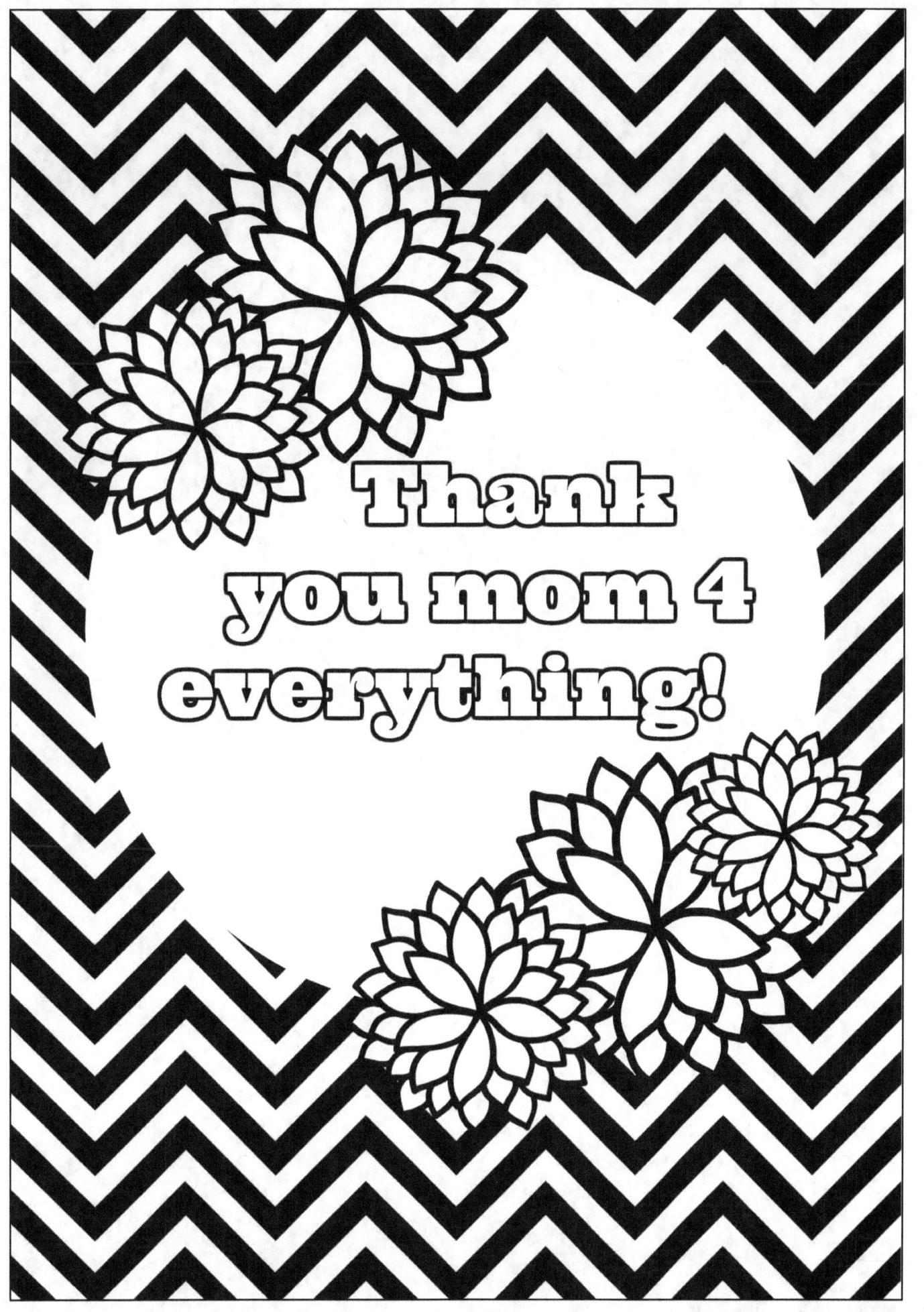